I *suppose* leadership
at one time meant muscles;
but today it means
getting along with people.

———

Indira Gandhi

Lore International Institute®
1130 Main Avenue
Durango, CO 81301

(970) 385-4955
Fax: (970) 259-7194

Printed in the United States of America

LTI-Gen-Man-112008

Leadership
through
INFLUENCE

by Terry R. Bacon, PhD

LORE®
INTERNATIONAL INSTITUTE
A KORN/FERRY COMPANY

CONTENTS

Introduction		**6**
Core Concepts of Influence		**8**
Section 1	**POWER AND INFLUENCE**	**11**
	Influence Model	13
	Influence Techniques	14
	Influence Strategies and Techniques	16
	Negative Techniques	17
	Power Base	19
	Technique, Power, and Skill Correlations	20
Section 2	**INFLUENCE TECHNIQUES**	**23**
	Legitimizing	25
	Logical Persuading	29
	Appealing to Relationship	33
	Socializing	37
	Consulting	41
	Stating	45
	Appealing to Values	49
	Modeling	53
	Exchanging	57
	Alliance Building	61
Section 3	**SOURCES OF POWER**	**65**
	Role	68
	Resources	69
	Information	70
	Network	71
	Reputation	72
	Knowledge	73
	Expressiveness	74
	Character	75
	Attraction	76
	History with the Influencee	77
	Applying Power Directionally	78

Section 4   **APPLYING POWER AND INFLUENCE 79**
Understanding the Situation   81
Understanding Operating Styles   82
The Myers–Briggs Type Indicator®   83
Recognizing the Types   84
Influencing Different Types   87
Influencing by Temperament   90
Influencing Directionally   92

Section 4a DOWNWARD INFLUENCE   **93**
Creating an Empowered Environment   95
Delegating   98
Coaching and Mentoring   101
Applying Power and Influence   104
Power Sources in Downward Influence   105
Downward Influence Techniques   109

Section 4b UPWARD INFLUENCE   **113**
Understanding Your Boss   115
Understanding Yourself   116
Building a Working Relationship   118
Applying Power and Influence   120
Power Sources in Upward Influence   121
Upward Influence Techniques   125

Section 4c LATERAL INFLUENCE   **129**
Assessing Lateral Influencees   131
Building Relationships   132
Applying Power and Influence   135
Power Sources in Lateral Influence   136
Lateral Influence Techniques   139
Understanding Lateral Exchange   145
The Currencies of Lateral Exchange   146

Assessing Your Influence Effectiveness   **149**
Recommended Readings   **150**
Index   152

INTRODUCTION

Influence occurs when one person's will prevails over another person's will, however temporarily. There are many examples of influence:

- You persuade a customer to purchase a product or service.
- A colleague agrees to help you on a project.
- Your boss agrees to a change in procedure when you show him or her a better way.
- A subordinate agrees to redo work you felt was not accurate.
- Based on your arguments, a team agrees to shift priorities.
- While speaking to a group, you convince a number of people to adopt a quality program.

Unethical Influence

Some people react negatively to the idea of influence. They may be thinking of "influence peddling," which is unethical and illegal. But influence is not necessarily unethical. In fact, in many instances, it is the only way to accomplish something. Influence is persuasion, and so long as the other person agrees, of his or her own free will, to be persuaded, you are influencing with integrity.

However, there are numerous examples of influencing that is unethical, immoral, or illegal:

- Someone tries to extort money by threatening violence.
- Someone manipulates a situation so that you have no choice but to agree to do what he or she wants.
- Someone lies to you and gets you to act on false information.
- Someone bullies or intimidates through greater size or power.
- A manager demands sexual or other favors and threatens loss of job if the subordinate declines.
- Someone who should make a decision won't do so and forces others to act blindly.

These are cases of influencing without integrity. They constitute reprehensible behavior and should always be avoided. Except to point out such types of negative influence behaviors, this manual will not deal with them. Instead, we will focus on how you can influence others *with integrity*.

Why study influence?

In the 1970s, the world entered the Information Age, and with it came a new way of doing business. Organizations found that, to remain competitive, they had to tap what Jack Welch of GE called "the reservoir of talent and creativity and energy that can be found in each of our people."

Hierarchy and bureaucracy are giving way to flatter, more responsive organizations that stress the involvement and commitment of employees at all levels. Leadership and influence can no longer rely on the mantle of authority, on the power relationships that have existed between managers and employees.

Today, business people, at all levels, must rely on their ability to influence others in order to accomplish important organizational results.

Influencing on automatic

Most of us influence on automatic. That is, we aren't aware of the techniques we're using. When we succeed, the other person (the influencee) is being reasonable. When we fail, we often attribute our failure to the influencee's ignorance or unreasonableness. Our language provides some convenient excuses: The influencee "doesn't see the light" or "can't see the forest for the trees." It's easy to attribute our failure to the other person.

We also tend to overuse the influence techniques we are comfortable with, even when it's clear they aren't working. We sometimes try to use logic, for example, and when we meet resistance to our logic, our natural impulse is to pile on more facts and figures. We seem to think that if a little logic isn't working, then the remedy is more logic. (In fact, if logic creates resistance, you should abandon logic and use another technique.)

Influencing consciously

The purpose of this manual is to help you become more aware of how people influence others with integrity. Specifically, it describes the ten common influence techniques and the sources of power you must have to be able to influence others.

Leadership through

Core Concepts of Influence

Here are some of the core concepts of influencing with integrity:

1. Influence is consensual.

In influence (as opposed to manipulation), the influencee consents to be influenced. In other words, he or she has the right to say no. This means that the person must be aware of your influence attempt and your motives. When influence is done with integrity, the influencee chooses to be persuaded but is fully aware of the option not to be.

2. Influence is situational.

Whether and how effectively you can influence someone depends on numerous factors, including the environment, the organizational and national culture, your relationship with the influencee, your power base, and your skill level. It also depends on the influencee's openness to different influence techniques and on the influencee's state of mind at any moment. Consequently, an influence technique that works under one set of circumstances may not work under other circumstances.

3. Influence is a process, not an event.

It is possible to influence people quickly, but influence usually occurs through a series of encounters over a period of time. Your ability to influence someone often develops over a period of repeated interactions, so you should not become discouraged if your first influence attempt fails.

4. Influence often involves a mixture of strategies and techniques.

In any single interaction, a person commonly uses a mixture of influence strategies and techniques. For example, one might begin an influence attempt by consulting and, upon being questioned by the influencee, use legitimizing or logical persuading to explain.

Influence techniques are rarely used by themselves. Usually, they occur in some logical combination, given the nature of the issue and the influencee. It's useful to think of influence techniques as working in combination, depending on the situation.

5. Influence is bilateral.

When we try to influence others, we need to be open to influence as well. Influencing with integrity includes listening and negotiating. We aren't simply imposing our will on others. Instead, we are "negotiating for consent." In effect, the influencee agrees to meet us halfway. Rarely is influence unilateral.

6. People respond best to the techniques they use.

The influence techniques people use most often are the ones they are comfortable with and find most persuasive themselves. Thus, to determine how to influence someone, notice how he or she tries to influence others, including you. The techniques the influencee uses are most likely to work on him or her.

7. People give cues that tell you how best to influence them.

Finally, influencees offer a number of visual and verbal cues that tell you what approaches to take. If you are listening and observing carefully enough, those cues will tell you which influence techniques are most likely to succeed.

How This Manual Is Organized

This manual has four sections.

SECTION 1 will introduce you to the concepts of power and influence and to the TOPS model, which will show you how power and influence are related.

SECTION 2 describes each of the ten common influence techniques in detail. Here you will learn how to recognize the techniques, how to read the cues that influencees give you, and how to use the techniques most effectively.

SECTION 3 describes the ten sources of organizational and personal power. Each of us must have some power sources in order to influence others.

SECTION 4 discusses how to apply power and influence. In particular, it shows you how to adapt your influence approach to different operating styles and how to influence upward, laterally, and downward.

We hope you enjoy it.

Leadership through

Power
&
INFLUENCE

POWER AND INFLUENCE

Influence effectiveness depends on three factors: using the right technique for the situation, having the right power base for the technique, and having the right skills to use the technique. These three factors work in combination and may be represented by the following formula:

$$TOPS = Result$$

T = Technique

Researchers have identified ten common techniques people use to influence others with integrity. In addition, there are four negative techniques.

We don't recommend using negative techniques because they are unethical and are usually detrimental to your relationship with the influencee. However, people do use negative techniques, so you should be aware of them.

O = Organizational Power

Each of us derives some power from the organizations we work for. There are five sources of organizational power: role, resources, information, network, and reputation. To some extent, we can influence others (inside and outside our organization) because of these power sources.

P = Personal Power

In addition, each of us has some power derived from our own capabilities and traits. There are five personal power sources: knowledge, expressiveness, attraction, character, and history with the influencee.

If you are in a powerful position in your organization, you can rely on organizational power sources; if not, you must depend on personal power sources. In either case, it is not possible to influence others without having some strong power sources.

S = Skill

Finally, each influence technique requires a unique set of skills, and your success depends on your proficiency in the skills associated with a given technique. The chart on page 20 shows the correlations between each positive influence technique and the power sources and skills. Understanding these correlations is a key to understanding how to influence others more effectively.

T	**O**	**P**	**S**
Techniques	**Organizational Power**	**Personal Power**	**Skills**
			Knowing rules
Legitimizing	Role	Knowledge	Logical reasoning
Logical persuading	Resources	Expressiveness	Writing
	Information	Attraction	Problem solving
Appealing to relationship	Network	Character	Valuing perspectives
Socializing	Reputation	History	Intuition
Consulting			Sensitivity to differences
Stating			Resolving conflicts
Appealing to values			Building rapport
Modeling			Flexibility
Exchanging			Asserting
Alliance building (macro technique)			Leading
			Determining values
Negative Techniques			Inspiring others
Avoiding			Negotiating
Threatening			Managing details
Intimidating			Speaking
Manipulating			Objectivity
			Interpersonal skills
			Consistency
			Empathizing
			Listening
			Engendering trust
			Innovating
			Questioning
			Persisting
			Motivating
			Managing meetings
			Coaching
			Managing teams

TOPS = Result

INFLUENCE

Power and

INFLUENCE TECHNIQUES

Following are brief definitions of the ten techniques in Lore's influence model.

Legitimizing

Using authority or credentials to explain and influence; showing that what you want is consistent with policy, procedure, or tradition; referring to the wishes or directives of management, to laws or rules, or to recognized authorities or experts; dropping names of others who support you.

Logical Persuading

Using logic or evidence to explain or justify a position; arguing logically or rationally; showing that yours is the most logical alternative; following a proven process to arrive at a decision or conclusion; relying on knowledge or expertise to give reasons; being analytical; providing facts, statistics, data, charts, graphs, photos, or other forms of proof to make a case.

Appealing to Relationship

Asking based on relationship; relying on family ties, group affiliation, friendship, loyalty, trust, or a past relationship to get what you want; asking for personal favors; doing favors; showing caring or willingness to help; telling colleagues that you need their help or are counting on their support; letting them know that they can count on you.

Socializing

Establishing a basis for asking; behaving in a warm and friendly manner so as to influence strangers to cooperate; being friendly, disclosing personal information, building a relationship; showing empathy; building rapport by identifying commonalities, matching behaviors, or pacing; complimenting or appealing to vanity.

Consulting

Asking the influencee to help you arrive at an acceptable solution; appealing to the influencee's expertise; asking for input, probing for feedback; collaborating; inviting the influencee to participate or become involved in a process; setting standards or making decisions jointly; incorporating the influencee's ideas, acting on his or her suggestions to provide ownership.

Stating

Simply saying what you want or what you think; making a direct statement; asserting your position; being confident, certain, or positive; leaving no room for negotiation; not wavering; insisting or demanding in a nonthreatening way, without suggesting punishment or other consequences.

Appealing to Values

Inspiring cooperation by appealing to the influencee's values, emotions, or feelings; showing enthusiasm, commitment, dedication, or passion; being impressive, motivational, or inspirational; telling stories; giving the big picture; painting an exciting or otherwise energizing picture; speaking in terms of achievement, quality, or other desirable values.

Modeling

Inspiring the influencee to behave in a certain way by setting an example; leading by example; behaving in the way you wish for others to behave; coaching, mentoring, or teaching; assessing performance, giving feedback; "walking through" something with the influencee; showing or demonstrating how to do something; encouraging the influencee.

Exchanging

Giving something of value to the influencee in return for what you want; negotiating, bargaining, or trading something; offering something with explicit or implicit expectations of reciprocity; reciprocating; exchanging favors or benefits; creating a win–win situation; compromising or making a concession in return for a concession; answering the question "What's in it for me?"

Alliance Building

Getting a number of people together, either to accomplish something you could not accomplish on your own or to influence another, more powerful, individual or group; building a network of supporters; extending your power base; finding commonalities or shared goals, emphasizing similarities and minimizing differences; building consensus; defining a group position; creating an us–them situation.

INFLUENCE
Power and

INFLUENCE STRATEGIES & TECHNIQUES

One way to remember the ten positive influence techniques is to think of them in terms of strategies: five strategies plus a macro strategy.

Explaining is the strategy of clarifying or giving reasons for what you want, using either of two techniques: legitimizing or logical persuading.

Asking is the strategy of making a request, using one of three techniques: appealing to relationship, socializing, or consulting.

Stating is the simple strategy of saying what you want or what you think. It is a technique as well as a strategy.

Inspiring means affecting behavior by emotion or example. In appealing to values, you use emotion to inspire; in modeling, you set an example.

Exchanging, like stating, is a strategy in itself. It means giving something in return for what you want.

Alliance building means getting more than one person on your side. To do this, you may need to use any or all of the other strategies~hence, the term *macro strategy*.

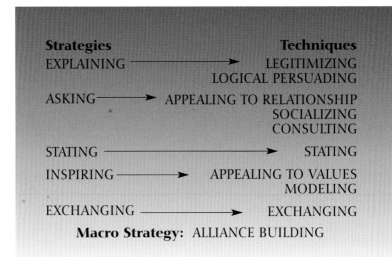

Strategies	Techniques
EXPLAINING ⟶	LEGITIMIZING
	LOGICAL PERSUADING
ASKING ⟶	APPEALING TO RELATIONSHIP
	SOCIALIZING
	CONSULTING
STATING ⟶	STATING
INSPIRING ⟶	APPEALING TO VALUES
	MODELING
EXCHANGING ⟶	EXCHANGING

Macro Strategy: ALLIANCE BUILDING

NEGATIVE TECHNIQUES

People sometimes use one of these four negative (or unethical) techniques:

Avoiding

Failing to act or respond; behaving passive-aggressively; appearing to acquiesce; creating excuses for not acting; ignoring or being silent when they should speak; reserving the right to say, "I told you so" (by not acting); delaying by procrastinating.

Threatening

Describing punishment or other negative consequences; expressing excessive anger toward another person; using power to inflict punishment or bring about negative consequences; stating or implying the ability to punish or cause physical harm; being physically aggressive; carrying, brandishing, or alluding to a weapon.

Intimidating

Using a size or power differential to get your way; invading another person's space; failing to acknowledge another person's presence or point of view; interrupting or otherwise not listening; being loud, overbearing, arrogant, or insensitive; taking advantage of an individual's minority status.

Manipulating

Withholding information; lying, deceiving, misleading, pretending, or disguising your feelings or intent; having a hidden agenda; allowing the other person to act without full knowledge; using an individual's weaknesses against him or her; playing upon fears.

Negative techniques can be influential, but they are not ethical and will probably damage the relationship with the influencee. We recommend that you never use these techniques.

Negative Techniques and Integrity

Influencing with integrity implies the influencee's awareness and consent to be influenced, either expressed or implied, as well as the influencer's willingness to be influenced. It also implies that the influencee has the right to say "no." If you influence someone without their knowledge or consent (as in doing something behind their back which denies them the right to exercise a choice), then you are not influencing with integrity. On the next page is a three-part test for influencing with integrity.

Power and

Negative Techniques

The Test of Integrity

1. Has the influencee consented to being influenced?
2. Is the influencer open to being influenced?
3. Does the use of the technique build and maintain the relationship?

All four negative techniques fail this test.

Avoiding fails the test of integrity because the influencer isn't open to being influenced. No give-and-take nor negotiation is possible because the influencer is not responding. The influencee is being forced into a position by the influencer's lack of responsiveness, rather than consenting to being influenced. Finally, the repeated use of avoidance will seriously damage or perhaps destroy the relationship.

Intimidating offers no choice to the influencee. The influencer only wants his/her way and is not open to being influenced. Intimidation creates resentment and damages the relationship.

Threatening fails the test for the same reasons as intimidating.

Manipulating fails the test because the influencee has not given consent and the influencer is not open to influence. The relationship may survive manipulation, but the manipulation does not actively build or maintain the relationship.

Countering Negative Techniques

Stating is an excellent approach to countering the negative techniques:

George, I feel that you've been avoiding this. Would you mind explaining . . . . (avoiding)

That sounds like a threat. If you carry it out, I will have no choice but to . . . . (threatening)

I'll be happy to talk this through with you if you'll take the seat on the other side of my desk . . . . (intimidating)

I need some assurance of _____ before I can act on this . . . . (manipulating)

A direct but nonconfrontational statement can head off the negative technique and provide you an opportunity to counter with another technique such as consulting or exchanging.

POWER BASE

Your power base consists of five organizational and five personal power sources. These vary in strength, depending on the situation and the influencee.

Organizational Power

These power sources are greater within an organization but are not necessarily confined to it.

- **Role**
  Your authority to make decisions that impact others' jobs

- **Resources**
  The extent to which you control the resources other people need

- **Information**
  Your access to and control of information

- **Network**
  The number of powerful people you know and your ability to get things done through these connections

- **Reputation**
  What others know or think of you

Personal Power

These power sources are based on the qualities and characteristics of an individual.

- **Knowledge**
  Your knowledge and expertise that others know of and respect

- **Expressiveness**
  Your ability to communicate

- **Attraction**
  The immediacy and extent to which others like you and are interested in what you have to say

- **Character**
  Others' perceptions of your honesty and integrity

- **History with the Influencee**
  The degree to which others have worked with you and know what to expect from you

You can build your power base over time. How-to's appear in Section 3, along with more detailed descriptions of these organizational and personal power sources.

Power and

TECHNIQUE, POWER, & SKILL CORRELATIONS

Each of the ten positive influence techniques has a set of relevant skills (see complete list on page 14 and 15) as well as a set of related power sources. To use the technique effectively, its related power sources must be high and you must be proficient in the skills that apply to a given influence situation.

INFLUENCE TECHNIQUE	RELATED POWER SOURCES	
Legitimizing	Role	Network
Logical persuading	Information Expressiveness	Knowledge
Appealing to relationship	Character History	Attraction
Socializing	Expressiveness	Attraction
Consulting	Reputation Attraction	Knowledge History
Stating	Role	History
Appealing to values	Reputation Character History	Expressiveness Attraction
Modeling	Reputation Character	Knowledge History
Exchanging	Resources Reputation Knowledge History	Information Network Expressiveness
Alliance building	Role Information Network History	Resources Reputation Expressiveness

RELEVANT SKILLS

Managing details	Knowing rules		
Managing details Problem solving	Logical reasoning Writing	Speaking	Objectivity
Interpersonal skills Empathizing	Valuing perspectives Sensitivity to differences	Intuition Listening Engendering trust	Consistency Resolving conflicts Building rapport
Interpersonal skills Empathizing	Building rapport Sensitivity to differences	Intuition Speaking Listening	Valuing perspectives Engendering trust
Interpersonal skills Flexibility	Innovating Sensitivity to differences	Intuition Empathizing Listening	Valuing perspectives Engendering trust Questioning
Asserting	Consistency	Persisting	Leading
Interpersonal skills Empathizing Inspiring others	Listening Leading Engendering trust	Intuition Determining values Speaking	Motivating Managing meetings
Coaching Persisting	Consistency Engendering trust	Inspiring others	Leading
Intuition Determining values Speaking Questioning	Negotiating Problem solving Persisting Motivating	Flexibility Managing details Listening Resolving conflicts	Asserting Innovating Valuing perspectives Engendering trust
Interpersonal skills Flexibility Speaking Building rapport Negotiating	Persisting Knowing rules Consistency Managing teams Engendering trust	Intuition Determining values Listening Resolving conflicts Innovating	Valuing perspectives Motivating Leading Managing meetings

Power and INFLUENCE

Influence
TECHNIQUES

INFLUENCE TECHNIQUES

Section 1 introduced ten techniques for influencing others with integrity. This section defines these in detail and describes how and when to use each technique.

Each of us is more comfortable with and more skilled in using some techniques than others. Furthermore, we tend to stick with what has worked in the past. Consequently, we develop a limited repertoire of influence skills.

To broaden your repertoire and become more effective at influence, you need to identify the techniques you use less frequently and less skillfully, and build your skills and confidence with these techniques. To use them effectively, you must understand how people are influenced and be sensitive to styles and preferences of others.

How People Are Influenced

To be effective at influencing others, you need to understand the following:

- Different people respond differently to the various influence techniques, so you can't use the same techniques with everyone. You have to use techniques an influencee will respond to, regardless of the technique you're most comfortable with.

- People tend to use the techniques they are most responsive to. *This is a key point.* It means that if I respond to logical persuasion, then I will try to use logical persuasion on others. One key way, then, to determine which influence techniques to use with an individual is to observe which techniques he or she tries to use on others.

How to Choose a Technique

Here are suggestions for determining which technique to use in a given situation:

- **Use the techniques the influencee uses.** Remember that people respond best to techniques they try to use. If you're observant enough, you can identify their preferred techniques and adopt them.

- **Listen and look for cues from the influencee.** If you listen and observe carefully, influencees will give you cues indicating how best to influence them. This section identifies the common cues for each technique.

- **Use techniques appropriate to the influencee's personality type.** Finally, different types of people respond to different techniques. Section 4 describes the different personality types and the techniques that generally work best for each type.

Legitimizing is using authority to influence. Authority includes organizational rules and procedures, laws, regulations, traditions, customs, and various symbols of authority (uniforms and badges as well as formal dress and environment). You can also legitimize by citing higher authorities.

Legitimizing strengthens your request with precedent, tradition, procedure, or other standard means of operating. Most people respect authority, so if you have rank (role power), legitimizing is the easiest technique to use. Legitimizing can be very quick, especially when influencing downward or when influencing a number of people.

How to Recognize This Technique

Legitimizing behaviors include:

- Using authority or credentials to explain and influence
- Showing that what you want is consistent with policy, procedure, custom, rules, or tradition
- Referring to the wishes or directives of management, to laws or rules, or to recognized authorities or experts
- Using the signs and symbols of authority
- Referring to others whom the influencee respects

LEGITIMIZING	
Power Sources	*Skills*
Role	Managing details
Network	Knowing rules
Supporting Techniques	*Conflicting Techniques*
Logical persuading	Consulting
Appealing to values	Appealing to relationship
Stating	Socializing
Alliance building	Threatening (too soon)

Influence

LEGITIMIZING

How to Recognize People Who Respond to This Technique

- They show respect for authority.
- When asked how something should be done, they refer to procedures, rules, or standard practices.
- They are currently (or have previously been) part of the armed forces, the government, or another organization governed by strong, hierarchical leaders or rules.
- They quote famous or respected people or otherwise show respect for powerful people.
- They talk about how things are done and use the word "should."

When to Use This Technique

- When you have the right to make the request and the influencee will perceive that you have that right.
- When your request is consistent with policy or procedures.
- When you have the support of higher authorities and can call upon them to back you up.
- When your organization has a formal enough system that people will respond to authority. The more formal and bureaucratic your organization, the more effective legitimizing will be.
- When you need quick compliance.
- When you need compliance from a number of people, especially subordinates.
- When your organization is having a crisis, and that crisis is broadly acknowledged and well understood. People tend to obey authority more readily in a crisis.
- When you cannot use appealing to relationship, socializing, exchanging, or another collaborative technique.

How to Use This Technique

1. Refer to policies, procedures, standard practices, tradition, strategic goals, or publications as the basis for your decision:

According to procedure, all engineering drawings should be submitted to . . . .

The policy manual says we're supposed to . . . .

Traditionally, the company has handled these situations by . . . .

We promise in our promotional literature to . . . .

2. Cite higher authority in making your request, either directly or indirectly:

I have written authorization from the Group Vice President to implement this plan, and I need your assistance in . . . . (direct request)

The director of manufacturing asked me to look into our use of polyvinyl. (indirect request)

3. Allude to higher authorities even if you don't have specific authorization to proceed:

In a speech to the Board of Directors last year, the CEO outlined four strategies . . . .

4. Make your initial request or a follow-up request in the presence of higher authority.

5. Drop names, but only in conjunction with the legitimate basis for your request:

During our meeting yesterday, the director said . . . .

I've asked our division manager about _____, and she said that . . . .

I've spoken to the department heads about my plan, and they've given tentative approval.

The vice president looked at my proposal and suggested I meet with you to discuss how we might implement . . . .

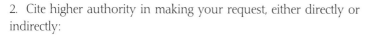

Influence

LEGITIMIZING

6. Establish rules, procedures, or protocols that others agree to follow. How? Try consulting (pp. 41-44). Most individuals will follow rules they helped to create.

7. Choose a formal or official setting, such as your office or a conference room, to make your request.

8. Speak authoritatively and confidently. Convey authority in your demeanor and self-presentation. People who act as though they have authority are able to exercise considerably more influence than they might otherwise have.

9. Use the signs and symbols of authority:
> Corporate logos/flags
> Uniforms or badges
> Formal dress
> Printed agendas/invitations

10. Gain support from higher authorities and get tangible evidence of their support (phone calls, memos, attendance at meetings, etc.). Sometimes a name on a distribution list is all it takes.

CAUTION: This technique will not work with people who, by their nature, resist authority.

CAUTION: Overusing this technique may cause resentment or resistance, or build an unfavorable reputation. Other techniques are often better, especially with peers.

CAUTION: If you have authority and are influencing downward, consider whether this is the right technique and whether any technique is necessary. Consider stating (pp. 45-48). Legitimizing may be necessary only if the influencee is questioning your authority. Instead of legitimizing, just make the request.

CAUTION: When using legitimizing to influence upward, make sure the influencee is congenial or at least can delegate the obligation to respond to someone with whom you have legitimate authority.

LOGICAL PERSUADING

Logical persuading is using logic, facts, evidence, data, and rational arguments to explain and influence.

Many people feel comfortable with this technique because it reflects the intellectual basis of the scientific revolution, and logical discourse is usually taught in schools. Education prepares people to accept logical arguments. In fact, people can be influenced by the mere appearance of logic. Appearance without substance is influential, too ~ in the opposite direction.

Logical persuading is inherently the least powerful of the influence techniques, because its psychological basis is logical, not emotional. Logical persuading is often ineffective when emotional issues or biases prevail. By and large, people don't make decisions logically. They make them emotionally and then justify them with logic. So be aware of the limitations of this technique.

LOGICAL PERSUADING

Power Sources	Skills	
Information	Managing details	Logical reasoning
Knowledge	Speaking	Objectivity
Expressiveness	Problem solving	Writing

Supporting Techniques	Conflicting Techniques
Stating	Appealing to values (if overused)
Appealing to relationship	Consulting
Appealing to values	Negative techniques
Modeling	
Exchanging	
Alliance building	

LOGICAL PERSUADING

As a general rule, if people are emotional, they do not use logical persuading. They won't listen to your logic. Also, if you are attempting logical persuasion and you're encountering resistance to the logic, then try another technique. Resistance to logic generally means that the other person is emotionally blocked from receiving the logical argument.

How to Recognize This Technique

Logical persuading behaviors include:

- Using logic or evidence to explain or justify a position

- Arguing logically or rationally

- Showing that yours is the most logical alternative

- Following a proven process to arrive at a decision or conclusion

- Relying on knowledge or expertise to present factual reasons; being analytical

- Providing charts, graphs, data, statistics, photographs, or other forms of proof to make your case

How to Recognize People Who Respond to This Technique

People who will respond to logical persuading usually have the following characteristics:

- They have an advanced degree, especially in a technical subject. Most people receiving advanced degrees have spent years studying logical thought processes.

- They are engineers, scientists, mathematicians, or otherwise work in a technical field.

- They prefer the word **think** to the word feel. They'll say:

    I think this is correct.
    I've thought about it and believe . . . .

- They ask for or respond well to data. They want concrete evidence to validate a point.

- They think and speak in terms of sequences and causality:

    What should we do first?
    I think A should precede B.
    What caused that to happen?

- They will ask for proof of your assertions:

    How do I know that's true?

- They get right to the point and are interested in facts and figures.

- They will try to use logic on you.

When to Use This Technique

- When the influencee shares your values and goals (and when rational arguments will not conflict with the influencee's values)

- When you have good persuasive skills and know how to use data to prove your point

- When the evidence supports you

- When the influencee is not emotionally committed to another outcome

- When you have expertise, information, or insights the influencee doesn't have

- When you are the expert and your organization is not in crisis ~ i.e., the situation does not demand a quicker response

How to Use This Technique

1. Prepare by working through the problem carefully and to ensure that your case is well thought out and supported. Examine your assumptions and anticipate the influencee's assumptions and objections.

2. Explain why you are making your request or proposing a course of action. Always say why. In and of itself, giving a rationale is influential.

Influence

LOGICAL PERSUADING

3. Provide evidence to support your conclusions. Charts, graphs, tables, models, statistics, and other forms of evidence are compelling. The more formal they appear, the more persuasive they will be.

4. Use evidence that the influencee is not aware of. New information bolsters your credibility.

5. Relate the current situation to previous situations that were resolved using the approach you're recommending. If the influencee contends that the previous situation or results are not applicable to the present, show how they are applicable.

6. Empathize and probe for understanding if you sense emotional resistance. Use questioning to explore the emotional issues and work your way back to logic.

7. If the influencee defends an irrational position, shift to another technique. If the influencee needs more proof, go find it.

CAUTION: Logical persuading can be time consuming. If you need quick compliance, try another technique, such as legitimizing (pp. 25–28) or appealing to relationship (pp. 33–36).

CAUTION: Make sure your logic and evidence are sound. Don't risk destroying your credibility!

CAUTION: Don't try this if you think the influencee questions your competence. Consulting (pp. 41–44) might work better in this case.

CAUTION: Avoid arguments. Arguing is not persuasive; it's divisive and emotionally charged.

APPEALING TO RELATIONSHIP

Appealing to relationship (asking for assistance based on friendship or membership in a group) relies on the natural human tendency to help others with whom we feel some afinity.

We are inclined to grant the requests of people we like or feel similar to in some respect. We tend to do favors and to reciprocate when people do favors for us.

Some people are less comfortable and less successful with building and maintaining relationships, especially at work. Those people may be uncomfortable with the technique of appealing to relationship ~whether they are using it or someone else is using it on them. It may seem manipulative. Other people may be so comfortable with the technique that they overuse it.

Used with the right people, appealing to relationship is a very powerful influence technique~in fact, it is the most powerful technique of all.

APPEALING TO RELATIONSHIP

Power Sources	Skills	
Attraction	Interpersonal skills	Valuing perspectives
Character	Intuition	Consistency
History	Empathizing	Sensitivity to
	Listening	differences
	Resolving conflicts	Engendering trust
	Building rapport	

Supporting Techniques	Conflicting Techniques
Logical persuading	Legitimizing
Socializing	Stating (if overused)
Consulting	Exchanging (if overused)
Appealing to values	All negative techniques
Modeling	
Exchanging	
Alliance building	

Influence

Appealing to Relationship

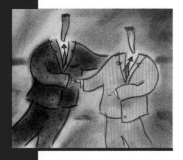

How to Recognize This Technique

Appealing to relationship includes the following behaviors:

- Asking based on an existing relationship
- Relying on friendship, loyalty, trust, or a past relationship to get what you want
- Asking for personal favors; doing favors
- Showing caring or willingness to help
- Telling family, colleagues, teammates, or friends that you need their help or are counting on their support
- Letting them know that they can count on you

How to Recognize People Who Respond to This Technique

This technique only works with people with whom you already have a close relationship, so recognizing them is easy. Nonetheless, look for the following characteristics:

- They are friendly and seem inclined to be helpful, whether or not you ask for help.
- You know the person well enough to know that asking for help or asking for a favor will not be perceived as inappropriate.
- Your relationship is one of mutual trust. Both of you know that neither one will violate that trust or take advantage of the other.
- You know the person well enough to know how to repay the favor without the other person having to ask for it.
- You have a long enough history with the person to know what to expect from him or her and vice versa.

Appealing to relationship is based on trust and on a long history with the influencee. It's the most powerful technique to use because most people are less willing to say no to people they feel close to.

When to Use This Technique

- When you have an established relationship with the influencee
- When you need whatever it is right away
- When the influencee is likely to cooperate based on your relationship alone
- When you have little to exchange
- When you can't use stating
- When influencing downward and appealing to relationship will not compromise your authority
- When influencing upward and you have a good relationship with the influencee
- When your request will not compromise or jeopardize the influencee
- When the influencee owes you a favor
- When you won't be compromised by the obligation to reciprocate

How to Use This Technique

1. Ask for help if you have a collegial relationship with the influencee:

   Juan, I need a little help on this analysis. Would you do me a favor and identify . . . .

2. Recognize and acknowledge any inconvenience your request may cause the person and be sensitive to his or her needs in return:

   I'm sorry to impose on you, Sarah, but I need your help. I owe you one.

3. Consider doing something for the influencee first. People who receive a favor usually feel a sense of obligation.

4. State how important the cooperation is and how much you're counting on their support.

5. Be willing to reciprocate.

6. Continually build the relationship by showing genuine interest, caring, and concern. Share information about yourself. Stop by to say hello. Invite the other person to lunch. Let the other person know that you consider him or her a friend, that you care about more than what he or she can do for you in business.

CAUTION: Be careful with this technique (it might seem like you're using your friends). Doing an unexpected favor and then asking for a favor in return can appear manipulative, particularly if you do it often. Most people will decline a request for a favor if they perceive that you have a hidden motive.

CAUTION: Avoid appealing to relationship if the other person would be at risk by complying.

SOCIALIZING

Socializing, like appealing to relationship, is based on the natural human tendency to help people we like or feel similar to. When we aren't friends with someone, we can socialize. Socializing brings people closer and establishes common ground. It sets the stage for asking for assistance, if not now, then at some point in the future. Socializing is unique among influence techniques in that you don't need a specific influence goal to use it, and using it  builds influence. If you're a friendly, outgoing person, you use it every day, without thinking about it. All those with whom you socialize are more likely to cooperate with you in the future. Socializing is a powerful technique by itself, but it also increases your success with the other influence techniques.

How to Recognize This Technique

Socializing behaviors include the following:

- Behaving in a warm and friendly manner so as to influence strangers to cooperate

- Being friendly, disclosing personal information, building a relationship

SOCIALIZING

Power Sources	Skills	
Expressiveness	Interpersonal skills	Building rapport
Attraction	Intuition	Valuing perspectives
	Empathizing	Sensitivity to differences
	Speaking	Engendering trust
	Listening	

Supporting Techniques	Conflicting Techniques
Consulting	Legitimizing
Appealing to values	All negative techniques
Alliance building	
Stating	

Influence

Socializing

- Showing empathy
- Building rapport by identifying commonalities, matching behaviors, or pacing
- Offering ideas, establishing a give-and-take
- Complimenting the other person sincerely or otherwise appealing to that person's vanity

Some people consider socializing to be insincere and manipulative. However, it doesn't have to be. Many people socialize effectively all the time. The key is sincerity. If you do it sincerely and genuinely, socializing is an effective interpersonal technique and a powerful influence technique.

How to Recognize People Who Respond to This Technique

People who respond well to socializing are usually very social themselves. They will exhibit these characteristics:

- They will be friendly and outgoing when you meet them, or they will respond well to your attempts to be friendly.
- They tend to be expressive and people oriented.
- They are similar to you in some fashion (same school, same hobbies, same tastes, etc.).
- Their office is full of personal knick-knacks or mementos. They display aspects of their personal life (almost inviting you to ask them about it).
- They are joiners and are interested in talking about people.

When to Use This Technique

- When you do not have an existing relationship with the influencee but would like to build one
- When the influencee seems receptive
- When making friends is easy for you
- When you have no authority over a lateral influencee and can't use other techniques
- When you have little leverage and little to exchange laterally
- When you're working on a team and need to establish relationships with other team members
- When influencing downward and using this technique will not compromise your authority
- When you encounter a gatekeeper, in an unfamiliar organization, and need that person's help

How to Use This Technique

1. Introduce yourself in a friendly, open manner. Extend your hand. Volunteer some information in addition to your name:

Hi, I'm Susan Bradley, second-year Sales Associate.
I'd heard you'd come on as our new . . . so I thought I'd
stop by and introduce myself.

2. Build your knowledge. Find out about the things that people like to talk about so you'll be able to converse with them in their territory. Even if you're not interested in a particular subject ~ say, sports ~ make a point of keeping up on selected teams and players. Learn and remember just enough to get by in a conversation.

3. Use verbal and visual matching behaviors, also known as pacing, to build rapport. Speak the other person's language. Mirror the other person's posture, gestures, and attitudes without mimicking them.

Socializing

4. Show an interest. Ask others about their interests. Get them talking about what they know or what they like to do.

5. Listen actively. Make frequent eye contact. Nod, encourage, reflect. Ask questions.

6. Remember and use names and other details in conversation. Nothing is more powerful than remembering names and other personal facts about someone you've just met. People are very influenced by that.

7. Identify and talk about the things you have in common:

> *I've heard you're a graduate of Harvard Business School. I've been reading John Kotter's new book. Did you know him?*

8. Talk about your interests. Disclose personal information, but not too much. Mention important people in your life and things you like to do outside of work. The other person will pick up on commonalities.

9. Empathize. A person who is having a hectic time or a bad day will do just about anything for someone who notices and makes a sympathetic comment.

10. Use socializing on the telephone as well as in person.

CAUTION: Socializing, like appealing to relationship, can easily backfire if you're not sincere.

Consulting is influencing through collaboration ~ inviting the influencee to contribute to the concept, proposal, approach, plan, or strategy. When people contribute to the plan, they feel some ownership of it and will therefore be more committed to it. Consulting, basically, means asking for input and then combining the input with your ideas to form a joint plan the other person will support.

You can also use consulting by *asking* for someone's advice on solving a problem and then asking or encouraging them to implement their suggestions. This form of consulting is especially effective when senior people use it with more junior people. It rarely works the other way around.

How to Recognize This Technique

Consulting behaviors include the following:
- Asking the influencee to help you arrive at an acceptable solution
- Appealing to the influencee's expertise
- Asking for input, probing for feedback
- Collaborating

CONSULTING

Power Sources	Skills	
Reputation	Interpersonal skills	Innovating
Knowledge	Intuition	Valuing perspectives
Attraction	Flexibility	Sensitivity to
History	Empathizing	differences
	Listening	Engendering trust
	Questioning	

Supporting Techniques	Conflicting Techniques
Appealing to relatioinship	Legitimizing
Appealing to values	Logical persuading
Logical persuading	(if overused)
Alliance building	Stating (strongly)
Socializing	
Stating	

CONSULTING

- Inviting the influencee to participate or become involved in a process
- Setting standards or making decisions jointly
- Incorporating the influencee's ideas, acting on his or her suggestions to provide ownership

How to Recognize People Who Respond to This Technique

People who respond well to consulting are people who want to be part of the solution ~ in other words, most people. But those who are especially responsive have these characteristics:

- They have advanced degrees and may prefer to be called by their titles: *Doctor, Colonel, Professor, etc.*
- They have previously been involved in similar projects or have dealt with this topic before.
- They are senior to you and may resent other influence techniques.
- They seem proud of their knowledge or expertise and show, in some way, that they want to contribute ideas.
- They offer unsolicited advice:

  What you ought to do is . . . .
- They are proud, arrogant, or overbearing and always seem to have a better way to do something.
- They display their awards and honors conspicuously (framed certificates on the walls, etc.).

When to Use This Technique

- When the influencee has special knowledge, information, or resources that you need
- When you lack confidence in your input on its own
- When you need to build a broad base of support
- When the influencee perceives that the outcome is important to him or her
- When your success hinges on the influencee's support or when the influencee has the power and potential for negative impact
- When participation is the only way to gain cooperation
- When you honestly value the influencee's input
- When the influencee's ego is an issue or is at stake
- When your boss refuses to delegate
- When developing a plan that your subordinates will have to implement
- When subordinates would benefit from participation
- When you need to build enthusiasm and goodwill

How to Use This Technique

1. Formulate your own proposal, concept, or plan, and state it in broad terms that allow the influencee latitude in offering advice or assistance.

2. Be genuine in asking for the influencee's assistance and ideas. If your request does not seem genuine, you may lose the person's trust and could damage the relationship.

3. Identify the problem and your own assumptions clearly. Then state exactly what you need from the influencee.

CONSULTING

4. Listen carefully as the influencee responds. Ask open questions to stimulate more information (What other factors should I consider?) and closed questions to clarify (So you see a merger as the best choice?).

5. Ask leading questions to direct the influencee's attention to the areas you want to focus on:

Should we try the other approach?

How would this alternative affect the cost of production?

6. Use the influencee's ideas to form a synergistic plan or proposal that integrates your ideas and the influencee's ideas. Be sure the influencee knows this.

CAUTION: Don't invite criticism unless that's what you want, and don't invite more feedback than you need. Clearly define what you want from the influencee when consulting.

CAUTION: Consultation may create an expectation of future consultation. Don't undermine your own power base by overusing consulting.

CAUTION: Be honestly open to input from others, and avoid using consulting to manipulate.

CAUTION: Make sure you give appropriate credit to those whose ideas you solicit through consulting.

STATING

Stating is the simplest influence technique of all. It means, simply, saying what you want or what you think.

Stating can be used to accomplish a broad spectrum of influence goals, from everyday asserting to pressuring. It can be used laterally, downward, and (with caution, in limited circumstances) upward.

Stating also works well in team settings and is one of the best ways to resist influence.

How to Recognize This Technique

The following behaviors are characteristic of stating:

- Making a direct statement of need or opinion
- Asserting a position
- Being confident, certain, or positive
- Leaving no room for negotiation
- Persisting, not wavering
- Insisting or demanding in a nonthreatening way, without suggesting punishment or other consequences

STATING		
Power Sources	*Skills*	
Role	Asserting	Consistency
History	Persisting	Leading
Supporting Techniques	*Conflicting Techniques*	
Legitimizing	Appealing	Avoiding
Logical persuading	to values	Manipulating
Appealing to relationship	Modeling	Consulting
Socializing	Exchanging	(if overused)
Consulting	Alliance building	

Influence

Stating

How to Recognize People Who Respond to This Technique

Most people respond to stating. Those who are most responsive have these characteristics:

- They are not, by nature, argumentative. If someone takes a firm stand, they are likely to accept it.
- They are under considerable pressure. (Most people under pressure need to make quick decisions and will respond well to a firm position that seems to allow for no debate.)
- They have a full schedule. (If you don't pressure them, you may not wind up high enough on their priority list.)
- They use stating themselves. People who often use stating are comfortable with taking a stand and are more likely to respect someone else doing the same.

When to Use This Technique

- When you need quick compliance
- When influencing subordinates
- When influencing laterally or upward and resistance is unlikely
- When you have no authority, no relationship to appeal to, or little to exchange with a lateral influencee
- When an upward influencee is a person who appreciates straightforwardness
- When you have authority or some form of leverage
- When the situation is potentially negative and you're not ready to threaten
- When you're in a focused crisis (one that the influencee understands and accepts)
- When you're working on a team where you need to maintain your voice and visibility
- When you need to refuse or object

How to Use This Technique

1. Make a polite but direct statement of what you want:

   Please sign this requisition.

2. Assert your position with confidence and self-assurance:

   I am qualified and up to the challenge.

3. Do your homework. Provide enough facts to substantiate your statement, but no more:

   Your salary and benefits are already in the top third of the competitive range for this area.

4. Anticipate and address potential arguments:

   I realize that you've already worked a lot of weekends, but this project has to be finished by Monday. That means you'll need to work this weekend.

5. Leave no room for negotiation or refusal. Avoid tentative phrases like I think, I feel, I was hoping you would, if you don't mind, etc. Don't phrase your statement as a question (would you mind, don't you agree, can I ask you, etc.). Resist the urge to be overly polite or apologetic.

6. Demand in a nonthreatening way:

   This proposal has to go out on Friday. I've got to have your review comments by tomorrow morning.

7. Use strong verbals. Speak firmly and concisely, without over-qualifying. Be polite, but powerful:

   Excuse me, Susan, but we'll never come up with a plan that's within budget if you're not willing to compromise.

   I can't support your proposal without some concession in the area of . . . .

Influence

STATING

8. Use assertive body language:
   - Maintain eye contact
   - Stand or sit erect, with shoulders squared
   - Lean slightly toward the influencee
   - Use broad, expansive gestures
   - Use your voice and gestures for emphasis

9. Use stating as a way to resist negative influence techniques:

   Bob, you keep interrupting me.

   Please let me finish. I'd feel more comfortable, Louis, if you'd take the chair on the other side of my desk.

   I suppose you'll have to carry out that threat, then, because I cannot. . . .

   Your continual references to cultural stereotypes bother me, Frank, and make me less receptive to your suggestions.

10. Use stating as a way of saying "no." If you have trouble with a direct "No," then find a subtler way to say it:

    I'm afraid I can't because . . . .

    I'd do it, but I've made prior commitments.

    Thank you for the offer, but I wouldn't enjoy it.

    Maybe some other time.

11. When the situation is unpleasant or has the potential to become unpleasant, use stating before threatening, intimidating, or avoiding. Negative circumstances often arise out of misunderstanding. Clearly stating your needs, wishes, or intentions helps to eliminate misunderstanding.

> CAUTION: Don't substantiate or explain too much. If you do more than the minimum, you're using logical persuading.
>
> CAUTION: Don't overdo the force with which you state. Stating that is too strong can become negative techniques, threatening or intimidating. The idea is to be firm but not to bully.

APPEALING TO VALUES

Appealing to values is a way to influence people based on their values, feelings, and emotions. You make such an appeal by conveying a strong vision (of excellence, achievement, etc.) or by presenting your case with enthusiasm and conviction:

We can achieve our goals if we believe in ourselves and set our own standards higher than anyone expects us to.

If used well, this technique can be highly influential, and it can reach a number of people at once. It's good for stimulating extraordinary efforts. However, it takes great skill to do it well, especially on a mass level.

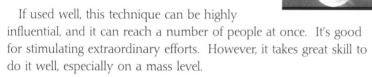

APPEALING TO VALUES

Power Sources	Skills	
Reputation	Interpersonal skills	Listening
Expressiveness	Intuition	Motivating
Character	Empathizing	Leading
Attraction	Determining values	Managing meetings
History	Inspiring others	Engendering trust
	Speaking	

Supporting Techniques	Conflicting Techniques
Appealing to relationship	Logical persuading
Socializing	Legitimizing
Consulting	All negative techniques
Modeling	
Stating	
Alliance building	

APPEALING TO VALUES

How to Recognize This Technique

The following behaviors are characteristic of appealing to values:

- Inspiring cooperation by appealing to the influencee's values, emotions, or feelings

- Showing enthusiasm, commitment, dedication, or passion

- Being impressive, motivational, or inspirational

- Telling stories to illustrate values

- Painting an exciting or otherwise energizing picture, especially the big picture

- Speaking in terms of achievement, quality, or other desirable values

How to Recognize People Who Respond to This Technique

To some extent, all of us respond to this technique. It's the rare person who isn't responsive to a talk by an inspirational speaker if we share the speaker's values and are interested in the topic. However, those of us who are most responsive have these characteristics:

- They use words that indicate high values, words like *achievement, quality, customer service, etc.*:

  Our most important goal is to serve our customers, to deliver excellence in every product we sell.

- They prefer *feeling* words to thinking words:

  It doesn't feel right to me.

  I feel that our best course of action is to . . . .

- They belong to religious, social, or fraternal organizations that aspire to higher ideals or serve a common interest.

- They tend to be social and enthusiastic, as opposed to people who are solitary and analytical.

- They quote famous people or read books by inspirational writers.

- They become energized by topics that interest them. There is often a marked change in their demeanor when the conversation shifts to a topic of interest. When that occurs, their gestures and speech become more animated.

When to Use This Technique

- When you have a strong vision of your goal and feel driven to achieve it
- When your goals and values are consistent with the goals and values of those you wish to influence
- When your attraction, expressiveness, and other power sources are very strong
- When you need support outside of your functional area, and larger organizational goals or values justify that support
- When you need to influence many people at once
- When you need support for an innovative proposal
- When you need to improve performance, reinvigorate commitment, reverse a trend, implement a major change, or issue a challenge
- When you need to persuade someone (especially a subordinate or a group of subordinates) to accept a difficult task or assignment
- When you need a subordinate to devote more time and energy to something
- When you need to stimulate an extraordinary effort

APPEALING TO VALUES

How to Use This Technique

1. First, build trust and a common ground with the people you want to influence. You must know and share their values.

2. Evaluate your own vision, convictions, and values. Unless you feel strongly about the issues, you will not succeed using this technique. You must be inspired first.

3. Appeal to the influencee's higher values:

   • Loyalty to the organization

   • Making a contribution

   • Participating in a cause

   • Serving a larger purpose

   • Excelling

   • Defeating a common enemy

   • Being part of a winning team

4. Use signs, symbols, images, metaphors, rituals, and ceremonies to give the appeal a larger-than-life feeling.

5. Convey enthusiasm and conviction; stress the value of accomplishing the goal, and express confidence in the other person's abilities. Use stories, parables, and anecdotes to communicate values.

6. Always behave in a manner that is consistent with your vision. You must be a role model for what you are proposing.

7. Listen to what the influencee values and then use those values in your message. For instance, if the person values excellence, then frame your message in terms of achieving excellence.

CAUTION: Don't be insincere in appealing to values, and be sure that your appeal is consistent with the influencee's values.

CAUTION: Don't trying appealing to values with a group unless you have strong speaking skills.

MODELING

Modeling is a way to show people what you want, either by behaving in the manner you wish for them to behave or by demonstrating the actions you wish them to take.

Modeling is an important influence technique in organizations. Most managers try to model behaviors they want their direct reports to emulate. You often see examples of modeling in the way managers dress, in their responsiveness, in their work ethic, etc. Obviously, some managers do not model positive behaviors in these areas, and they often suffer the consequences of their counter-examples.

Modeling is very powerful when influencing downward. It also works well laterally and upward. Because everyone is susceptible to peer pressure, colleagues may begin to emulate behavior or actions that bring positive results. An executive, noticing those results, may recognize the behavior and direct broader implementation.

Modeling is an effective follow-up technique to appealing to values. Through modeling, you show your ongoing commitment to the goals and values you espoused in your original appeal.

MODELING		
Power Sources	*Skills*	
Reputation	Coaching	Consistency
Knowledge	Inspiring others	Leading
Character	Persisting	Engendering trust
History		
Supporting Techniques	*Conflicting Techniques*	
Appealing to values	Consulting	
Stating	Avoiding	
	Manipulating	
	Intimidating	

TECHNIQUES

Influence

MODELING

Modeling is also the most effective way to transfer your knowledge and skills to someone to whom you need to delegate. Many people learn best by doing. Unfortunately, they can't always do it on their own the first time. They need a coach, a mentor ~ someone to show them how. By helping them through the first time, you not only ensure a job well done; you also build a better relationship.

How to Recognize This Technique

The following behaviors are characteristic of modeling:

- Inspiring the influencee to behave in a certain way by setting the example
- Leading by doing and demonstrating the right way
- Behaving in the way you wish for the influencee to behave
- Coaching, mentoring, or teaching; assessing performance; and giving feedback
- Walking through something with the influencee
- Showing or demonstrating how to do something
- Providing encouragement

How to Recognize People Who Respond to This Technique

People who are responsive to modeling have these characteristics:

- They are responsive to advice or guidance. When given advice, they seem receptive to it (as opposed to people who appear to resist or resent it). They act on suggestions or solicit feedback.
- They ask for guidance or assistance; they ask questions or appeal to your experience or expertise.
- They sign up for courses, study on their own, or attend lectures.
- Relative to your role, they are in a subordinate or student role.
- They have an "accepting" personality. They are not strongly independent, cynical, or skeptical.
- When people who are recognized authorities speak, they take notes or ask questions.

When to Use This Technique

- When you need to sustain commitment to goals or values

- When you are in a position of leadership

- When you want to be taken seriously as a leader

- When you need to set standards or change behavior

- When you want to increase your visibility, either laterally or upward

- When you need to transfer your knowledge or skills to someone else

- When the task is large and/or the stakes are high

How to Use This Technique

1. Use modeling as your primary leadership tool. Model the values of the organization. Treat others with respect, empathy, sensitivity, and consideration. Show a positive attitude. Provide encouragement and rewards. Work hard. Let integrity guide your interactions with co-workers as well as clients. Adhere to quality standards. Set an example. Communicate your expectations by living up to them in front of others. Make your self-development plans and goals public. Be punctual. Keep your commitments. Follow through. Stick to your schedule; meet your deadlines. Deliver as promised.

2. Don't publicize the fact that you are modeling; just do it.

3. Recognize those who emulate what you model not for emulating your behavior, but for the behavior itself. Give recognition as if the person being recognized, not you, had done the modeling.

MODELING

4. Be a coach and mentor. Share your knowledge and experiences. Be accessible and supportive. Give constructive feedback. Encourage and reward accomplishments. Allow people to learn from failure. Provide challenges.

5. To show an influencee how to do something for the first time or how to do it correctly, work alongside the individual. First, "walk through" the task or assignment. As a team, decide who will do what. Provide some hands-on, supervised training. Step aside when the person is ready to perform the task or complete the assignment on his or her own.

CAUTION: Failing to "practice what you preach" will damage your reputation and impair future attempts at influence through modeling.

WHAT VALUES TO MODEL

- That the enterprise is worthwhile and important
- That each person is worthwhile and important
- That goals can be achieved
- That the vision is not only attainable but a reality
- That the values are right
- That obstacles can be overcome
- That . . .

QUALITY	CUSTOMER
EXCELLENCE	SERVICE/
SPEED	SATISFACTION
SIMPLICITY	CARING
GLOBAL PERSPECTIVE	VALUE ADDED
DIVERSITY	EMPOWERMENT
CHANGE	TEAMWORK

. . . are priorities

EXCHANGING

Exchanging is trading something of value for the influencee's support or cooperation. In other words, it is negotiating as a form of influence. You ask a person to do something for you and offer an incentive:

If you'll support my reorganization proposal during the next meeting, I'll work over the weekend on your financial analysis and have the figures for you on Monday.

Exchanging can stimulate agreement when the influencee is otherwise ambivalent about your request, and it can build mutually beneficial relationships.

To be successful at exchanging, you need to have something to exchange, something of value to the influencee. (See "The Currencies of Lateral Exchange," Section 4c, pp. 146-148. Many of these currencies can be used in upward and downward exchanges. See also "Power Sources in Downward Influence," Section 4a, pp. 105-108, and "Power Sources in Upward Influence," Section 4b, pp. 121-124.)

EXCHANGING

Power Sources	Skills	
Resources	Intuition	Negotiating
Information	Flexibility	Asserting
Reputation	Determining	Problem solving
Network	values	Innovating
Knowledge	Managing details	Persisting
Expressiveness	Speaking	Valuing perspectives
History	Listening	Motivating
	Questioning	Engendering trust
	Resolving conflicts	

Supporting Techniques	Conflicting Techniques
Legitimizing	All negative techniques
Logical persuading	
Appealing to relationship	
Stating	
Alliance building	

TECHNIQUES

Influence

EXCHANGING

How to Recognize This Technique

The following behaviors are characteristic of exchanging:

- Giving something of value to the influencee in return for what you want
- Negotiating, bargaining, or trading something
- Offering something with explicit or implicit expectations of reciprocity
- Reciprocating
- Exchanging favors or benefits
- Creating a win-win situation
- Compromising
- Making a concession in return for a concession
- Answering the question "What's in it for me?"

How to Recognize People Who Respond to This Technique

Exchanging is a collaborative technique, so everyone responds to it to some degree. A number of people dislike overt exchanging and feel that it is unethical or manipulative. However, research indicates that most of us use exchanging, at least subconsciously, as a way to reach agreement when the other person is not compelled ~ by some other means ~ to agree with us.

People who are most responsive to exchanging have these characteristics:

- They use the language of negotiation and compromise:

  What if you were to . . . ?

  Can we agree on . . . ?

  How about if I . . . ?

- They use expressions like win-win and seek collaborative solutions.
- They control resources or have a background in resource management; their role involves handling requests or making assignments. (Such people are forced to exchange and become comfortable with it.)

- They talk about deals they've made:

  You should have seen the deal I got on that new car.

- They need something that you have, or they are responsive to intangibles, such as praise or recognition.

- They have a strong sense of obligation. When someone does them a favor, they feel compelled to repay the debt.

- They are borrowers. They frequently need something from others or often ask for help, advice, or resources.

When to Use This Technique

- When the influencee is ambivalent or resistant toward your request, plan, or proposal

- When you don't have a relationship to appeal to

- When the influencee values at least some of what you have to offer (resources, information, expertise, cooperation, recognition, assistance, etc.)

- When you have no authority or other leverage

- When the influencee has something that you need and is willing to trade it

- When you need to influence across functional lines or in several directions at once

- When you need to build interdependent networks

- When you control information or other resources that other people need

- When your boss depends on you to provide some critical resource and is not a heavy-handed authoritarian

- When influencing downward in an organization where hierarchical relationships are de-emphasized

- When exchanging with a subordinate will not compromise your authority or create unrealistic expectations (i.e., establish bargaining as the standard or preferred method of interaction)

EXCHANGING

How to Use This Technique

1. Find out what the influencee's needs, values, and interests are. Then formulate an exchange that will satisfy him or her. If you don't understand the "currencies of exchange," your negotiating may be ineffective. These currencies typically include resources, support, quick responses, information or expertise, and gratitude.

2. Think *win-win*. Avoid taking advantage, especially if the influencee is in a weaker negotiating position.

3. Make the benefits of the exchange evident if the influencee seems reluctant to negotiate. Clarify what's in it for him or her.

4. Seek a compromise solution if the person can't grant your request as it is. Find some way to make it easier for the person to say "yes."

5. Make your exchange offer explicit if you don't have a relationship with the influencee:

> *In return for the information I need, I'll agree to put together a list of marketing directors whom you could call for advice on managing advertising costs.*

6. Follow through on what you agree to do in exchange for assistance or support. If you don't reciprocate, you will quickly lose credibility.

CAUTION: Avoid having hidden agendas. Exchanges are built on trust. Don't manipulate!

CAUTION: Avoid exchanges with friends who might consider explicit negotiating to be a violation of the relationship. Appeal to relationship (pp. 33–36) instead.

ALLIANCE BUILDING

Building an alliance extends one's network and therefore builds
one's power base. An alliance can be an end (the result of
influencing a number of people needed to make a decision or
accomplish something you could not do on your own) or a means to
an end (expanded power to influence another, possibly more
powerful individual or group). Alliance building has great value and
is often necessary in organizations, particularly those with fewer
boundaries and more empowered individuals.

To build an alliance, you need to influence several individuals,
which may require that you use a number of other influence
strategies and techniques. In building an alliance, you may use
consulting with one individual and exchanging with another. You
may be able to persuade one individual to join the alliance by
appealing to relationship, whereas with another, you may need to use
logical persuading or even legitimizing. Because it involves many
individuals and influence techniques, alliance building is called a
macro technique.

ALLIANCE BUILDING

Power Sources	_Skills_	
Role	Interpersonal skills	Persisting
Resources	Intuition	Valuing perspectives
Information	Flexibility	Knowing rules
Reputation	Determining values	Motivating
Network	Speaking	Consistency
Expressiveness	Listening	Leading
History	Building rapport	Managing teams
	Resolving conflicts	Managing meetings
	Negotiating	Engendering trust
	Innovating	
Supporting Techniques		_Conflicting Techniques_
Legitimizing	Stating	Legitimizing
Logical persuading	Appealing	(if overused)
Appealing	to values	All negative techniques
to relationship	Modeling	
Socializing	Exchanging	
Consulting		

Influence

ALLIANCE BUILDING

An alliance can be more or less official. You don't have to say, "I'm building an alliance and I'd like you to join it." Instead, you may discreetly build the alliance through a series of one-on-one contacts, letting prospective allies know that you need their support and possibly mentioning who else is on board.

Alliances can be hard to form. They require time and energy to maintain. However, members of successful alliances tend to be more receptive to future alliances.

How to Recognize This Technique

The following behaviors are characteristic of alliance building:

- Getting a number of people together, either to accomplish something you could not accomplish on your own or to influence another, more powerful, individual or group

- Building a network of supporters

- Extending your power base

- Building consensus

- Finding commonalities or shared goals, emphasizing similarities and minimizing differences among individuals

- Defining a group position

- Creating an us-them situation

How to Recognize People Who Respond to This Technique

Alliance building may seem to be a collaborative technique, but in fact it's closer to legitimizing. It's using social pressure to compel someone to accept a position or grant a request. Clearly, some people are more responsive to this than others. Those who are most responsive to alliances have these characteristics:

- They worry about what other people think, and they may ask about it:

  Have you spoken to Charley? What does he think about it?

- They are joiners. They tend to belong to social or fraternal organizations.

- They are broadly networked and may refer to other people they know.

- They respect others' opinions and are particularly influenced by what senior people think.
- They are strong team players. They will talk about the importance of teams and the necessity to work together.

Be aware that some people resist alliances. They are highly independent and may become hostile or angry if you try to use an alliance to influence them. If sharp resistance occurs, try another technique.

When to Use This Technique

- When your organization is experiencing a diffuse crisis (one that is not well understood) and many heads are needed
- When you can identify potential allies who share your vision and goals
- When a longer response time is necessary or desirable
- When critical expertise is spread among several people
- When your power is limited and you need to magnify your power and influence through an alliance
- When you expect and will need to overcome resistance from selected individuals or functional groups
- When lateral or downward influencees must implement the plan
- When the influencee is at a higher level in the organization
- When the influencee requires proof of broader support
- When colleagues have much to contribute
- When you don't want to be solely responsible
- When your organizational culture favors participative management and empowerment over authority or hierarchy
- When you need to influence a number of subordinates across functional lines
- When building an alliance of subordinates will increase their enthusiasm

Influence

ALLIANCE BUILDING

- When influencing downward and building an alliance will not undermine your authority

How to Use This Technique

1. Ensure that prospective allies agree with your purpose or at least have something to gain by helping to achieve it.

2. Get one or more powerful or highly visible people on board first. Others will be more likely to join the alliance.

3. Create advisory groups, task teams, technical panels, etc. If you can, give these alliances some visibility and prestige.

4. Mix the power base. Include some people with legitimate authority, some recognized experts, etc.

5. Use logical persuading, consulting, exchanging, appealing to relationship, and other techniques to influence and gain the support of prospective allies.

6. Actively maintain the alliance. Don't assume that once on board, always on board.

CAUTION: An alliance that is built to influence a single, more powerful individual can appear mutinous. Before "ganging up" on someone ~ your boss, in particular ~ try other, less threatening techniques.

CAUTION: Beware of conflicts between allies that could damage the alliance and subvert your efforts.

Sources of
POWER

SOURCES OF POWER

Power is derived from one's personal attributes and position in an organization, and is largely in the mind of the beholder. In other words, your power often depends on how others perceive you.

Each of us who belongs to a business or professional organization derives some power from our role in the organization and the resources to which our role provides access. We also derive some power from personal sources, such as our knowledge and ability to communicate.

The amount of power available to you is the sum of your organizational and personal power. This power base is always relative and can be built over time. While you may not be able to increase some power sources ~ i.e., you usually can't promote yourself into a more powerful position ~ you can take steps to increase your power base. Pages 68-77 include suggestions for building the sources of organizational and personal power.

Sources of Organizational Power

These power sources are greater within the organization but are not confined to it.

- **Role** (p. 68)
  The power you derive from your position in an organization

- **Resources** (p. 69)
  The extent to which you control the resources other people need

- **Information** (p. 70)
  Your access to and control of information

- **Network** (p. 71)
  The number of powerful people you know and your ability to get things done through these connections

- **Reputation** (p. 72)
  What others know or think of you

The five sources of organizational power act in combination, and you can see how much power they give people in executive positions. These people have not only role authority, but also control of resources, access to information, a potentially broad network, and a powerful reputation (based on name recognition and perhaps high esteem). Someone like Jack Welch of

General Electric thus has considerable organizational power and is consequently quite influential ~ both within General Electric and in the international business community as a whole.

Sources of Personal Power

These power sources are based on the qualities and characteristics of an individual.

- **Knowledge** (p. 73)
  Your knowledge and expertise that others know of and respect

- **Expressiveness** (p. 74)
  Your ability to communicate effectively and make yourself understood

- **Character** (p. 75)
  Others' perceptions of your honesty and integrity

- **Attraction** (p. 76)
  The immediacy and extent to which others like you and are interested in what you have to say

- **History** (p. 77)
  The degree to which others know you and what to expect from you

To some extent, each of us has all of these sources of power. However, the strength of those power sources varies considerably ~ from person to person, situation to situation, and moment to moment.

With personal power sources in particular, power is in the mind of the beholder. Influencees grant us power based on their perceptions of us and the differences between their power sources and ours. So the amount and type of power you have depends in large part on whom you are trying to influence.

Power is relative and can be grown over time. In this section, we will suggest some ways to build each of your power sources.

Page 78 lists the power sources that are generally most useful in lateral, downward, and upward influence attempts.

Power
Sources of

ROLE

Role power refers to the power you derive from your position in the organization. It includes the following elements:

- Status, position, or authority
- The ability to make decisions affecting others' work or careers, to control assignments or work flow
- The power to reward or punish
- The ability to give or withhold recognition, promotions, or favors
- The extent to which one is indispensable to another, regardless of formal authority

Role power is based on the authority the organization grants to a position. Consequently, managers and executives usually have more role authority. However, anyone who is placed in a decision-making position will have a certain amount of role power that derives from the kinds of decisions that person can make and the impact of those decisions on others. Generally, the greater the impact on others, the greater the role power.

How to Build This Power Source

- Seek positions of greater authority.
- Study the formal systems and rules of your organization, comply with them, and insist that others do as well.
- Acquire the trappings of authority (degrees, titles, awards, etc.).
- Dress and act authoritatively.
- Learn to speak with confidence, expertise, and commitment.
- Start rewarding others for their contributions, support, and achievements.
- Try to join teams that make promotion, compensation, or assignment recommendations or decisions.
- Provide assistance or information to others as a reward for their support.
- Create rewards or other special symbols of merit and award them to deserving others.

RESOURCES

Another element of organizational power derives from your control of resources or other organizational assets. It includes the following elements:

- Control of important resources such as people, schedules, space, equipment, tools, budget, etc.

- The ability to give or withhold resources, thereby impacting other people's ability to accomplish their tasks.

People with tremendous resource power can be inordinately influential in their organizations. For obvious reasons, this is an extraordinary power source. For one thing, it is a key element in exchanging, where you must have something to exchange. People who control resources often become very good at negotiating and wield considerable power through their ability to give or withhold resources.

Interestingly, this is one power source that is often delegated to middle or lower levels of an organization. While managers may control budgets, other resources are often in the hands of mid-level people, who thus gain power through their control of resources.

How to Build This Power Source

- Seek positions that control resources.
- If possible, build your pool of resources ~ acquire more people, space, equipment, budget, etc.
- Increase your chances of gaining resources by publicizing the accomplishments of your team.
- Share your resources less freely (i.e., increase scarcity).
- Share your resources with those who share theirs with you.
- When you trade resources, clearly define the terms of the trade ~ i.e., the usage of your resources.

Power
Sources of

INFORMATION

A key organizational power source is access to information. Information tends to flow differently to different levels and functions within an organization. Because of this variation in the flow of information, this power source varies, depending on whom you are trying to influence and the types of information to which both you and the influencee have access.

Information power includes the following elements:

- Access to, control of, ability to disseminate information or data

- Possession of information that others need to do their jobs

- Possession of privileged or scarce information

- The ability to help or hurt others with information

How to Build This Power Source

- Gather and disseminate more information.

- Read more; read in your spare time, set aside time to read at work; pass along articles of interest to people who could benefit from them.

- Study unusual sources of information.

- Acquire and use information of importance to those you wish to influence.

- Create an information-rich job environment that others are aware of and need; use your network to gain information others would value.

- When asked for information, provide some value added (i.e., more than the minimum). However, don't inundate people with facts. Be selective. Show them what's important.

- Provide information, but don't make your information sources widely available (i.e., don't become a librarian).

- When you run across someone who could be helped by what you know, share it.

Another source of organizational power is that of network ~ i.e., access to others inside or outside the organization, the breadth of one's contacts, and the ability to engage others in important activities. The larger and broader the network ~ and the number of key people in it ~ the stronger your network power.

Network power includes the following elements:

- Access to information, resources, etc., through inside or outside contacts
- Committee/task force assignments, professional associations, political contacts
- The ability to get things done, possibly sidestepping processes, through "connections"

How to Build This Power Source

- Build a network of colleagues and peers within your organization; actively maintain the network by providing and soliciting information, support, feedback, and assistance.
- Socialize with co-workers whenever appropriate; have lunch, throw parties, join work-sponsored sports teams, etc.
- Accept invitations from others.
- Join professional associations and maintain your contacts within those associations.
- Seek assignments to task forces and committees within the organization.
- Become involved in political, charitable, or other civic groups.
- Stay in touch with your outside contacts.
- Introduce your friends and business associates to one another; make connections for others, and they will do the same for you.

Sources of

REPUTATION

Finally, organizational power comes from one's reputation. This refers to how much awareness others have of you and how much esteem they grant you. Name recognition and esteem are powerful indeed.

Reputation power includes the following elements:

- Others' awareness of one's knowledge, expertise, talents, abilities, or personal attributes
- Renown, fame, respect, recognition, or acclaim within an organization or industry

Reputation comes from published accounts of your accomplishments but also ~ and most importantly ~ from word of mouth within your organization:

He was very helpful to me on that project. If you ever get a chance to work with him, ...

She's an expert in this area. If you have any questions, . . .

Reputation depends on others' awareness of you in the organization and the esteem they have for you. Doing excellent work is the best way to develop this important power source.

How to Build This Power Source

- Cultivate impeccable work habits; do impeccable work.
- Get an advanced degree from a prestigious university.
- Accept speaking invitations.
- Publish in professional or scholarly journals.
- Develop your skills and expertise ~ attend seminars, training sessions, etc.
- Share your expertise with others; join teams and be a strong contributor.
- Take advantage of opportunities to make others aware of your little-known talents or expertise.
- Use your network to make contacts with others of high reputation.
- Don't "blow your own horn," but try to be recognized for your accomplishments.

The power that comes from knowledge is self-evident (as Sir Francis Bacon said, "Knowledge is power.").

This power source includes the following elements:

- Knowledge and expertise in a particular subject
- Procedural knowledge ~ i.e., how to get things done or how things work in an organization
- The ability to apply knowledge or share it with others to solve a problem or help others do their jobs

The power of knowledge has two important components. First, others must be aware of your knowledge; they must know that you know what you know. Second, your knowledge must be ~ to some extent ~ special or unique. You may be an excellent accountant, for instance, but if you're in a group of other excellent accountants, all of whom know what you know, then you will not have knowledge power.

To have high knowledge power, you must have some special expertise that sets you apart from others in your organization ~ and others must be aware of that special expertise.

How to Build This Power Source

- Expand your knowledge in critical areas through self-study, education, and training.
- Seek assignments that increase knowledge and experience through on-the-job experiences.
- Share your knowledge with others or use it in a way that lets others recognize your expertise.
- Acquire the evidence of knowledge (e.g., titles, degrees, special equipment).
- Learn and speak the jargon of an area of expertise.
- Seek opportunities to apply your knowledge to solve important problems.
- Seek membership on teams or committees where your expertise is recognized.
- Use your knowledge to further the organization's goals, and ensure that your expertise contributes to achievement of important organizational goals.

Power Sources of

EXPRESSIVENESS

Perhaps less evident than the power of knowledge is the power of expressiveness, which may be defined as effectiveness at communicating. It includes persuasiveness but is more than that. Expressiveness is the ability to express oneself, to convey ideas forcefully and clearly, to communicate effectively ~ both verbally and nonverbally. The more expressive you are, the more able you are to convey your point of view in a manner that others find compelling. Low expressiveness diminishes the power of even the most expert people.

Expressiveness includes the following elements:

- The ability to persuade by being articulate, expressive, enthusiastic, motivational, or inspirational
- Presentation or public speaking skills
- The ability to present information in a novel or interesting way
- The ability to communicate effectively
- The ability to facilitate, to promote dialogue, to bring people in or bring them together

How to Build This Power Source

- Develop your analytical and logical skills through education and training.
- Develop your writing and speaking skills and seek opportunities to speak before groups (e.g., join Toastmasters or a similar group that helps build your speaking skills).
- Present arguments factually, with concern for detail, supporting arguments, and evidence.
- Take an assertiveness training class.
- Seek feedback on your writing, speaking, listening, and overall communication skills.
- Study the techniques and approaches of expert speakers.
- Spend more time communicating. This may be difficult if you are shy or have a job in which you work in isolation, but the best way to become more expressive is to practice often. This is a key power source.

Character is a personal power source that lies, perhaps more than any other, in the mind of the influencee. The inclination of others to trust a particular individual ~ and, therefore, allow themselves to be influenced by that individual ~ hinges on their perceptions of the individual's character. Furthermore, perceptions of character are generally related to individual, highly personal definitions of character and to the relative values that different individuals place on given character traits.

Character includes the following elements:

- Trustworthiness, honesty, integrity
- Dependability and follow-through
- Loyalty, respect for others
- Personal ideals and values

How to Build This Power Source

- Clarify and adhere to your personal system of ethics and values.
- Practice what you preach; be known as someone who does what you say you will do.
- Follow through and keep your promises; don't make promises you can't keep.
- Don't make jokes at someone else's expense or talk about them behind their back. People with high character don't knock others down or try to win by causing someone else to lose.
- Show your loyalty; stand by others; don't be a "fair weather friend".
- Put your ethics and values above personal gain.
- Don't be manipulative. Let others know where you stand and what you want.
- Accentuate the positive; try always to have something good to say; avoid being cynical or pessimistic.
- Never show disrespect.
- Be honest in every interaction. Don't lie or distort information.

While this commonsense advice may sound like platitudes, the fact is, people who are perceived to have high character adhere to these principles.

Sources of

ATTRACTION

Attraction refers to the ability to draw others, attract them, and inspire a sense of commonality. Attraction is based on a number of interpersonal factors, such as genuineness, commonality of values, and sincere interest in others. Attraction might be defined as the ability to make friends. It is obviously a source of great personal power.

Attraction includes the following elements:

- Others' sense of affinity with or similarity to an individual
- Friendliness, genuineness, openness, willingness to disclose information about oneself
- Interest in others
- The ability to listen and empathize
- Charisma or magnetism

How to Build This Power Source

- Develop your interpersonal skills (supporting, listening, showing appreciation, being empathic, being considerate, finding common ground, etc.).
- Be friendly with everyone; try to establish a broad circle of friends.
- Support the efforts of others; be there when they need you.
- Accept others; don't judge or try to change them.
- Study the people you work with; know what motivates and inspires them.
- Study leadership, and exercise your leadership skills at every opportunity.
- Develop and articulate your personal vision.
- Speak enthusiastically; be animated and sincere.
- Be optimistic, self-confident, and energetic.
- Be a mender, not a divider. Seek to bring people together, to resolve issues, solve problems, etc.
- Take a genuine interest in and socialize with others. Genuinely listen to them; people are attracted to others who listen to what they have to say and are genuinely interested in their issues.

The final source of personal power is one's history with the influencee. An individual with a positive relationship, one whom the influencee knows well and feels he or she can trust, is much more influential than someone who is unknown.

History with the influencee includes the following elements:

- The extent to which one individual knows or has worked with another

- One individual's level of comfort with another

- The degree to which others know what to expect ~ i.e., consistency, predictability

- Willingness to work together, work things out, do favors, etc.

This is a source of power because we are more likely to be influenced by people we have known for a long time, especially if the history and relationship are positive. Because we know what to expect from such people, we are more likely to be influenced by them. Even when the relationship is strongly negative, when hatred or enmity have built up, we may be influenced by them, perhaps in an ironic way. For example, if a person we have grown to dislike says he is joining a particular team, we may avoid the team for that reason ~ and this may be precisely what he wanted.

How to Build This Power Source

- Seek opportunities to work with people you haven't worked with before.

- Be consistent and fair in your dealings with people.

- Express your appreciation and let others know you'd like to work with them again.

- Say good things to others about those with whom you've worked.

- Welcome opportunities to work with inexperienced or unknown people, even those about whom you've heard negative comments.

- Take the opportunity to build strong, positive relationships with key colleagues. Try to work with them long enough to build a significant and productive history.

Sources of

Applying Power Directionally

Which power sources do you need to influence your boss? Your colleagues? Those whom you lead? While the answer depends to some extent on the situation, each of the ten power sources has a downward, upward, and lateral application. (See Sections 4a, 4b, and 4c for details.)

Some power sources are more useful when influencing in one direction than another. Those listed below in larger, bold print are generally the most useful for influencing in each of the three directions ~ upward, laterally, and downward.

Organizational Power Sources	Personal Power Sources
Role	**Knowledge**
Resources	**Expressiveness**
Information	**Character**
Network	Attraction
Reputation	**History**
Role	**Knowledge**
Resources	**Expressiveness**
Information	**Character**
Network	**Attraction**
Reputation	History
Role	**Knowledge**
Resources	**Expressiveness**
Information	**Character**
Network	Attraction
Reputation	History

Applying Power
&
INFLUENCE

APPLYING POWER & INFLUENCE

As you apply power and influence, you should consider three important factors:

- The situation and environment in which you are trying to influence someone
- The influencee's personality or operating style
- The influencee's relationship to you and the direction you're trying to influence ~ upward, lateral, or downward

This section discusses all three factors. Sections 4a, 4b, and 4c address upward, lateral, and downward influence attempts.

Situation

As noted in the Introduction to this manual, influence is very situational. It depends on the environment in which you are trying to influence someone, on your organization's culture, and on many other situational factors that determine whether your influence attempt will succeed. Influence is dynamic, and, though we can provide some guidance on doing it successfully, the result always depends on the situation.

Operating Style Differences

Because people are diverse and respond differently to the same stimuli, we have to consider a person's personality or operating style when considering how best to influence him or her. Fortunately, we can classify people's operating styles and identify the best ways to influence different styles. The model we use to determine operating styles is the Myers–Briggs Type Indicator®, which is described in this section, beginning on page 83.

Influence Direction

Finally, and most significantly, how you apply influence techniques depends on the direction in which you are influencing. If you're trying to influence your boss (upward), you would use a particular subset of the techniques. If you were influencing colleagues (laterally), you would use a different subset, and so on.

Some techniques work better with bosses than they do with subordinates, and vice versa. It's important to understand which techniques work best in which directions (see page 92, as well as Sections 4a, 4b, and 4c).

UNDERSTANDING THE SITUATION

Numerous aspects of the situation can affect your application of influence techniques:

- **Your organization's culture**

  Some organizations are more hierarchical and formal, where legitimizing would be a good technique; other organizations are more fraternal, team oriented, and informal, where alliance building and consulting might work best.

- **The level of stress in the environment**

  In more stressful situations, you can use techniques that require quick decisions and less deliberation, such as stating, legitimizing, and appealing to values. In less stressful environments, techniques that require more time might be best, such as logical persuading, alliance building, and socializing.

- **External factors affecting the influencee**

  External factors might include customers, media attention, labor issues, budgetary crises, product shortfalls, vendor problems, etc. Any of these factors might alter the way the influencee would normally respond. Often, you're not even aware of these factors.

- **The influencee's state of mind**

  Factors affecting the influencee's state of mind might include recent decisions affecting that person, bad news, personal problems or triumphs, negative relationships with boss or colleagues, illnesses, and numerous other factors. A person who's in a bad mood might react quite differently than someone who's had recent good news and is feeling more cooperative as a result.

- **The influencee's recent history with you**

  A key situational factor is the influencee's recent history with you and attitude toward you. Has the person been giving in a lot lately? Or does the influencee feel that you deserve a favor?

- **The power differential**

  Finally, the power differential between you and the influencee plays a large part in determining how willing that person is to be influenced by you.

UNDERSTANDING OPERATING STYLES

You may or may not be able to do much about the situational factors that affect an influence attempt, but you can vary your approach depending on your perception of the influencee's operating style.

Through the ages, many thinkers have tried to identify how and why people behave differently. Among them was Hippocrates, who identified four temperaments: Sanguine, Choleric, Phlegmatic, and Melancholic. Numerous modern schemes are based on essentially the same four categories. One of the most popular is the Myers-Briggs Type Indicator®, or MBTI®, which is described in greater depth beginning on the next page.

The MBTI is based on work by Swiss psychologist Carl Jung, who published a book entitled *Psychological Types*. A mother and daughter team, **Katharine Briggs** and **Isabel Briggs Myers**, took Jung's concepts and created the four-dimensional type matrix shown on the next page. They also created an instrument for determining one's operating style or type.

While this scheme, which allows for 16 different personality types, may seem complicated, it is actually a fairly simple scheme once you understand it. And it's quite helpful in determining how best to influence someone because the 16 types respond differently to the ten influence techniques. The charts on pages 88 and 89 show these differences.

To think about operating style, you don't necessarily need to consider all four dimensions of the MBTI at once. It's often helpful to consider only one dimension, such as Thinker/Feeler, at a time.

Nonetheless, using the MBTI types to determine which influence technique to use is a skill that takes time to build, so don't become disheartened if it seems too difficult at first. Practice on one dimension at a time until you find it easier to identify someone's MBTI preference, and use the charts on pages 88 and 89 to develop, over time, a better understanding of how to apply influence techniques to different MBTI types.

This manual contains limited information on the MBTI differences. For more information, please contact:

CPP, Inc.
1055 Joaquin Road, 2nd Floor, Mountain View, CA 94043
(800) 624-1765

THE MYERS-BRIGGS TYPE INDICATOR®

The Myers-Briggs Type Indicator is based on Jung's psychological types and is one of the most researched and validated tools of its kind. It assesses personality along four dimensions, as shown below. The MBTI can identify differences in operating style but should not be used to stereotype, evaluate, or appraise individuals. In fact, part of its appeal is that there are no right or wrong preferences.

As shown below, the MBTI looks at type along four dimensions, and one's type is a combination of four letters (e.g., INTJ, ESFP). Two of the dimensions (S/N and T/F) are called functions. They relate to the ways we perceive [by looking at facts (S) or possibilities (N)] and judge what we perceive [by making logical connections (T) or weighing the relative values and merits of the situation according to human concerns (F)].

These dimensions are opposed but not mutually exclusive. We embody some aspects of each dimension, but we typically prefer one function over its opposite. Similarly, we prefer either the extraverted or introverted attitude and the judging or perceiving orientation.

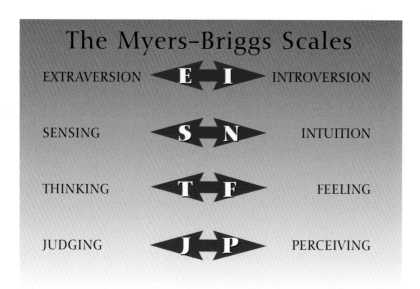

The Myers-Briggs Scales

EXTRAVERSION	**E** **I**	INTROVERSION
SENSING	**S** **N**	INTUITION
THINKING	**T** **F**	FEELING
JUDGING	**J** **P**	PERCEIVING

Applying Power &

RECOGNIZING THE TYPES

EXTRAVERTS

- Like variety and action
- Like to have people around
- Are often enthusiastic communicators
- Often think out loud
- Want to discuss topics before committing anything to paper
- Enjoy work that involves interacting with others
- Are typically action oriented; are uncomfortable with lengthy discussion

INTROVERTS

- Prefer quiet and time for concentration
- Are often drained by continuous interaction with others
- Like working alone
- Often prefer to write out ideas before discussing them
- May be reluctant to socialize
- Are more difficult to engage in sustained conversations
- Are often disturbed by interruptions

SENSORS

- Are practical and "down to earth"
- Are factual and are usually good detailers; they are concerned about the specifics
- Are concerned about what works and what's been proven
- Are often more comfortable fine-tuning something that already exists rather than trying something totally new
- Want to reduce risk
- Want to be shown why something makes sense
- Are typically more interested in applications than theory

INTUITORS

- Are oriented toward the future and toward possibilities
- May disregard facts or even make factual errors
- Prefer to think about the big picture
- Are typically more interested in theory than applications
- Enjoy learning new skills
- May seem restless and often work in bursts of energy
- Are visionary and follow their inspirations; may not be able to explain their rationale

THINKERS

- Are analytical and objective
- Tend to make impersonal decisions; may not consider the impact on people
- Focus on the principles behind the decision or plan
- Tend to be firm minded and may be critical
- Appreciate a well-organized presentation with points that are well supported
- May seem insensitive to others

FEELERS

- Are concerned about how decisions affect people
- May allow decisions to be influenced by what people like or dislike
- May have trouble delivering bad news to others
- Are often appreciative and personable
- May appear to be illogical or to value harmony over logical conclusions
- Will generally come across as being open and forthright
- Are often empathic and good listeners

INFLUENCE

Applying Power &

RECOGNIZING THE TYPES

JUDGERS	PERCEIVERS
• Want closure; want to get things settled and finished	• Are typically uncomfortable with tight deadlines
• Are typically very decisive, sometimes to a fault ~ making decisions too quickly	• Are flexible and adaptable
	• Prefer to leave things open and expect last-minute changes
• May become impatient with lengthy discussions that appear to be going nowhere	• Are open to exploring new approaches and alternatives to what's already been chosen
• Want to see things structured and scheduled	• Focus more on process than results and are more willing than Judgers to revisit the process and make changes to it if the process seems wrong
• Are often very good time managers and may insist that others be as punctual and controlled	
• Dislike surprises	• May postpone decisions in order to gather more information or search for more options
• Tend to be organized and to focus on the tasks to be done	
• Make and use "To Do" lists	• Are often uncomfortable with time management
• Are typically very orderly and organized	• Are usually spontaneous and will do things at the spur of the moment

INFLUENCING DIFFERENT TYPES

You will be more effective at influencing others if you adapt your use of influence techniques to their MBTI operating styles.

EXTRAVERTS

- Prefer action and interaction
- Use consulting, alliance building, appealing to relationship, and exchanging
- Never avoid or intimidate

INTROVERTS

- Prefer introspection and deliberation; want to know the impacts on them
- Use appealing to relationship and exchanging, but give them time to think about it

SENSORS

- Be factual with them; document successful applications
- Work out the details; show why it makes sense
- Use logical persuading, stating, and legitimizing

INTUITORS

- Give the global scheme
- Be confident and enthusiastic
- State challenges and future benefits
- Use appealing to values, exchanging, consulting, and modeling

THINKERS

- Be logical and organized
- State the principles involved
- List costs and benefits
- Use logical persuading

FEELERS

- Be personable and friendly
- State why it's valuable
- Use appealing to relationship/ values, consulting, modeling, and alliance building

JUDGERS

- Want to see decisiveness and closure
- Use legitimizing and logical persuading

PERCEIVERS

- Do not want to be pressured
- Use legitimizing, alliance building, consulting, and exchanging
- Never threaten or intimidate

Applying Power &

INFLUENCING DIFFERENT TYPES

	ISTJ	ISTP	ESTP	ESTJ	INTJ	INTP	ENTP	ENTJ
Legitimizing	◕	◕	◕	◕	○	○	○	◐
Logical persuading	◕	●	◕	●	◕	●	◕	●
Appealing to relationship	◐	◐	◐	◐	◐	◐	◐	◐
Socializing	◐	◐	◐	◐	◐	◐	◐	◐
Consulting	◐	◐	◕	◕	●	◕	●	◕
Stating	●	◕	◐	◕	◐	◕	◐	◕
Appealing to values	○	○	○	○	◕	◕	◕	◕
Modeling	◐	◐	◐	◐	○	○	◐	◐
Exchanging	◕	◕	●	◐	◐	◐	◐	◐
Alliance building	○	◐	◕	◐	○	○	◐	◐

LEGEND

○ Not likely to be effective under normal circumstances

◐ A **good** approach ~ but probably not your best choice

◕ A **better** approach to people of this type

● The **best** influence approach under normal circumstances

	ISFJ	ISFP	ESFP	ESFJ	INFJ	INFP	ENFP	ENFJ
Legitimizing	●	◕	◕	●	◐	◐	◐	◐
Logical persuading	◐	○	○	◐	○	○	○	○
Appealing to relationship	◕	●	◕	◕	◕	◕	◕	◕
Socializing	◕	●	◕	◕	◕	◕	●	◕
Consulting	◐	◐	◐	◐	◕	◕	●	●
Stating	◐	○	○	◐	◐	○	○	○
Appealing to values	◕	◕	◕	◕	●	●	◕	◕
Modeling	◐	◐	◐	◐	◕	◕	◐	◐
Exchanging	◕	◕	◕	◕	◕	◕	◕	◕
Alliance building	◕	◕	●	◕	◐	◐	◕	◕

LEGEND

○ Not likely to be effective under normal circumstances

◐ A **good** approach ~ but probably not your best choice

◕ A **better** approach to people of this type

● The **best** influence approach under normal circumstances

INFLUENCE
Applying Power &

INFLUENCING BY TEMPERAMENT

If you find the 16 MBTI types too complicated, one way to simplify it is to think in terms of the four temperaments. As noted earlier, the Greek philosopher, Hippocrates, identified four temperaments, which he associated with four fundamental personality types: Sanguine, Choleric, Phlegmatic, and Melancholic. These four temperaments are represented, more or less, by four groupings of MBTI characteristics, respectively: SF, ST, NT, and NF. Understanding these four temperaments can help you identify clear and simple differences in the techniques used to influence.

ST

Logical Persuading	Legitimizing	Exchanging
Stating	Consulting	

NOT Appealing to Values

SF

Legitimizing	Appealing to Relationship
Socializing	Alliance Building
Appealing to Values	Exchanging Consulting

NT

Consulting	Logical Persuading
Appealing to Values	Stating

NOT Legitimizing

NF

Appealing to Values	Consulting	
Alliance Building	Appealing to Relationship	
Socializing	Exchanging	Modeling

NOT Logical Persuading

ST — Practical and matter of fact

STs are factual and logical. To influence them, you must remain in the here and now and show that your plan or proposal has been logically thought out and is well supported with evidence that it will succeed. STs are most amenable to logical persuading. They also tend to respond well to legitimizing and exchanging (if it seems logical).

SF — Sympathetic and friendly

SFs are also practical, but they approach decisions with subjectivity and personal warmth. They tend to trust feelings, are more interested in facts about people than in facts about things, and ask how much something matters to themselves and others. Consequently, they are amenable to socializing, appealing to relationship, consulting, and alliance building (if their feeling side dominates). Appealing to values can also work.

NT — Logical and ingenious

NTs focus on possibilities, theoretical relationships, and abstract patterns. They are best at solving problems in pioneering areas, and they tend to subordinate the human element. They are influenced most by challenges and opportunities, so they respond well to appealing to values as well as to logical persuading (their logical side). Consulting also works because they want involvement.

NF — Enthusiastic and insightful

NFs focus on human possibilities. They are typically interested in the complexities of communication and are often superb communicators. They see the patterns underlying facts, symbolic meanings, and theoretical relationships. They tend to be very concerned about the impacts of decisions on people, and they want to involve others in planning. So they tend to respond well to consulting and alliance building, as well as appealing to relationship or values.

Applying Power &

INFLUENCING DIRECTIONALLY

A final factor to consider, along with an influencee's MBTI type, in selecting an influence technique is the direction of the influence attempt ~ upward, lateral, or downward.

All ten influence techniques can work in all three directions. However, certain techniques tend to work better with upward influencees, while others work better with lateral influencees and still others work better with downward influencees. Those listed below in larger, bold print are generally the best choices for influencing in each of the three directions.

The next three sections explain how to apply power and influence downward, laterally, and upward.

Consulting
Logical
Persuading
Exchanging
Alliance
Building
Modeling
Socializing
Appealing to
Relationship
Appealing to
Values
Stating
Legitimizing

Appealing to
Relationship
Socializing
Consulting
Exchanging
Logical
Persuading
Modeling
Alliance
Building
Appealing to
Values
Stating
Legitimizing

Modeling
Consulting
Alliance
Building
Appealing to
Values
Stating
Logical
Persuading
Exchanging
Legitimizing
Appealing to
Relationship
Socializing

Downward
INFLUENCE

DOWNWARD INFLUENCE

Influence is a process, not an event. Nowhere is this more obvious than in downward influence. Whether you are a traditional supervisor or a leader in some other capacity, your ability to influence those over whom you exercise leadership is cumulative. Direct reports and other downward influencees will be influenced as much by your day-to-day interactions with them as by any influence technique you may choose in a specific situation.

Downward influencees may include direct reports, indirect reports, those who report to your peers in other functional groups, and those with less seniority in the organization.

In an organization where cross-functional teams continually form and change with the workload, the lines of downward influence may continually change and vary from situation to situation. For example, you may find yourself on a team, taking direction from someone who is normally a downward influencee by virtue of a lower hierarchical position. In the team setting, however, this person becomes an upward influencee due to his or her team leadership position. In this situation, your ability to influence upward relies on your history with the influencee in the normal, downward role. Similarly, when downward influencees are promoted to positions higher in the hierarchy, they may become lateral influencees. Furthermore, your success with downward influencees is one of the keys to your success with both lateral and upward influencees.

These are the steps for downward influence:

1. Create an empowered environment for relationship building.

2. Build power and influence by delegating.

3. Be a coach and mentor.

4. Recognize the reciprocal nature of your relationships with subordinates and other downward influencees, and use your power sources and influence techniques wisely.

These steps are not linear, but concurrent and interrelated. Pages 95-97 offer suggestions for creating an empowered environment; pages 98-100, suggestions for delegating; and pages 101-103, suggestions for coaching and mentoring. Pages 105-112 list the downward applications of power sources and influence techniques.

CREATING AN EMPOWERED ENVIRONMENT

The best environment for relationship building between leaders and downward influencees is one of empowerment. True empowerment is sometimes difficult to achieve because, despite words and actions, many professionals may not feel truly empowered. In order to be empowered, they've got to feel empowered. Here are some ways that you, as a leader, can help to create the feeling of empowerment:

- **Expect self-management.**
  Expect people to take the initiative, solve their own problems, discover alternatives, analyze the situation, find solutions, and make decisions. If they don't, teach them how ~ but don't do it for them. Don't impose, dictate, or overrule.

- **Set high (but not impossibly high) standards of excellence.**
  People are more empowered when they feel that they're part of something extraordinary, so don't settle for adequate or even above average performance. Let the standards reflect better than above average performance.

- **Continually challenge people to exceed themselves.**
  High performers respond to challenges. Encourage them to stretch, to do even better than before.

- **Identify opportunities along with responsibilities.**
  People are empowered when they have a clear sense of their obligations and their latitude in solving problems and making decisions.

- **Create broad job descriptions.**
  Don't define roles more narrowly than you have to. Permit them the freedom to explore and grow.

- **Remove boundaries, real or perceived.**
  Rearrange the work area. Remove physical barriers that inhibit effectiveness. Minimize rules, restrictions, policies, and procedures.

- **Respect their space.**
  Let team members structure their personal work areas however they wish. Allow them to feel that their work areas, equipment, and supplies are their own. Avoid entering others' work spaces when they're not there, and when they are, apologize if you interrupt.

CREATING AN EMPOWERED ENVIRONMENT

- **Be accessible and aware.**
  Show that you're paying attention to them and their efforts regularly. You can't lead through absence or apparent indifference. Take an interest ~ and show it. Remember details. Make the rounds. Stay in touch. Practice what Tom Peters calls *MBWA ~ Managing By Walking Around.* Have an open door and an open mind.

- **Be an attentive listener.**
  Develop good listening skills. Lend an ear, and retain what you hear.

- **Give them the latitude to make decisions on how to accomplish their work, and make sure they know they have the latitude.**
  Some people, particularly those who have been working in hierarchical organizations and cultures, may not take initiative because they assume they're not supposed to. Challenge that assumption and let them know how much latitude they have.

- **Share more information.**
  Let them know more than they need to. Involve them in the bigger picture. Keep them up to date on organization, industry, and client developments and trends. If you happen to read an article in which a member of your team will have an interest, pass it along!

- **Help them develop networks.**
  Assign people to task forces. Hold information-sharing meetings or informal lunches with other groups. Send your people to conferences and industry gatherings. Introduce them to key people inside and outside the organization, and to clients and suppliers when they visit.

- **Let them participate in the decision making.**
  Form advisory committees or task forces to improve quality, customer service, internal procedures, etc. Give the committees a lot of visibility and rotate the memberships.

- **Seek and apply best practices.**
  Encourage and challenge your people to discover best practices, both in and outside the group. Reward people for better ideas.

- **Create peer mentors.**
  Encourage people to learn from one another, to train each other, and to share their skills and knowledge.

- **Create self-managing teams.**
  Form a team to achieve a specific goal, and let the team decide how best to go about it.

- **Create a "learning culture."**
  Model self-managed growth. Show them that you, too, are constantly learning and growing.

- **Provide access to resources.**
  Make sure your people have what they need to do their jobs well.

- **Help them build their skills and encourage self-development.**
  Provide the training necessary for them to build their skills and improve performance. Consider in-house training sessions given by your own people or people from other functional areas. Cross-training broadens skills and perspectives and builds flexibility.

- **Support people when they make mistakes.**
  Instead of blaming, look at the positive side and teach them how to avoid the negative side. Instead of telling them what's wrong, ask questions that lead them to discover problems for themselves.

- **Treat mistakes and failures as learning experiences.**
  When people falter, allow them to learn from the experience. In serious cases, reveal one of your failures and talk about your experience. Encourage them to learn from theirs and to try again.

INFLUENCE Downward

DELEGATING

Delegation is one of the best tools of leaders because it increases their own power and freedom while developing those to whom they delegate. Yet delegation is a tool that most leaders are reluctant to put into full practice and one that few leaders use well.

Delegation, if used well, increases influence with subordinates and other downward influencees in that it shows the leader's confidence in their abilities and commitment to their development. For the leader, delegation builds two important power sources: resources and history. The added resource power can be used laterally and upward as well as downward. For the delegatee, it builds history with an upward influencee and knowledge power, which can be used in lateral and upward influence. Here are some suggestions for practicing this "win-win" kind of delegation:

- **Seek buy-in and feedback from those to whom you delegate.** Whenever possible, delegate tasks to the people who want to do them. Ask them how they feel about what you've delegated. Try asking team members for suggestions, and consider delegating even the tasks you don't want to delegate to those who express an interest.

- **Delegate some of the risk and potential for rewards along with responsibility.** Delegate more than just the "grunt work." Include work that enhances visibility and value, work that presents challenges and risks.

- **Be sure they understand the *what, who, when, where, how,* and *why*.** Set the standards, define the process, and provide all of the resources to complete delegated tasks. Be very clear about the expected results. Show examples and provide the tools to do the job right. Set a deadline with an appropriate number of intermediate reviews. Be sure to state the purpose and benefits of the task.

- **The first time you delegate a difficult task, make it a "team effort."** Invite a team member to help you complete a task, with the eventual goal of assuming full responsibility for the task.

- **Show those to whom you delegate that you have faith in their abilities.** Express confidence that they'll be able to do it ~ even if it's a big stretch ~ and then, for the most part, leave them alone.

- **Offer your help, and be available if it's needed.**
Encourage those to whom you delegate to ask questions as they
arise or to seek your help if they get stuck. If the task is
particularly difficult, let them know that you'll be checking, and
then ~ as unobtrusively as possible ~ ask how it's going.
- **Publicly give credit for what you've delegated.** When
team members successfully complete delegated tasks, thank and
congratulate them in front of others. Let your leaders know that
you've delegated and, as appropriate, invite those to whom you've
delegated to join you in meetings or allow them to present their
work on their own.
- **Resist the temptation to do it yourself if it needs to
be redone.** If delegated work doesn't meet your expectations,
show the person what needs to be changed and let him or her,
not you, redo it.
- **Be willing to spend time on the front end.** Recognize
that delegation offers responsibility along with freedom. Take the
time to ensure mutual understanding, train properly, and develop
true competence. Trade the time you have to spend now,
explaining and instructing, for the time you *won't* have to spend
later, doing. Regard delegation as a means to achieve those
"challenging but achievable" goals.

If you're hesitant:

- **Challenge your own assumptions.** Ask yourself: Do I
really have to do this myself? Am I the only person who can do
it? What will I lose by delegating? What will I gain? What will
the work group gain? Examine the factors affecting your
willingness to delegate (see chart, next page).
- **Set a mandate for yourself to delegate.** If necessary,
make delegation one of your goals. Examine the factors affecting
your willingness to delegate, weigh their relative importance, and
regularly take reasonable risks with delegation. The successes may
surprise you!

DELEGATING

Factors Affecting Your Willingness to Delegate

Less Delegation ⟷ **More Delegation**

Less Delegation		More Delegation
Narrow	Leader's span of control	Broad
Low	Trust and confidence in team member	High
High	Leader's expertise/experience	Low
Low	Team member's expertise/experience	High
Low	Team member's availability	High
Low	Team member's willingness to accept responsibility	High
High	Leader's need for power and control	Low
High	Leader's interest in the task	Low
High	Deadline pressure	Low
High	Importance/criticality of task	Low
High	Degree of risk	Low

COACHING AND MENTORING

As a leader, you are in a position to help others grow, to model the values and behaviors they should emulate, and to provide the coaching and mentoring they need to develop their skills and self-confidence.

Coaching implies periodic or situational interactions, whereas mentoring implies more of a long-term, sustained commitment to the coaching role. The decision to be a mentor depends, of course, on the needs of individual downward influencees (usually direct reports) as well as your own feelings and availability. Below and on the following pages are some suggestions for coaching and mentoring.

Coaching

Coaching is one of the most powerful ways leaders can help others grow. Here are some suggestions for doing it well:

- **Provide coaching whenever it's needed, but also schedule time for one-hour coaching sessions.**
  New people might need coaching once a week or once a month; others once a quarter.

- **Determine what people need coaching in.**
  They generally don't need it in technical areas as much as they do in areas related to interpersonal effectiveness ~ communication, assertiveness, professionalism, conflict management, and so on. If you're in doubt, ask them what they need.

- **While coaching, focus on behaviors, not traits.**
  Focus on what they can change and what you can observe. Give feedback on how their behavior is impacting effectiveness. Then suggest alternative behaviors. Where possible, model the behaviors or otherwise show them how it's done.

- **Try to determine how they learn best and then match their learning style.**
  If they learn best by reading, give them reading materials; if they learn best by observing, then show them; if they learn best by doing, then arrange for them to practice.

COACHING AND MENTORING

- **Keep attending to your coaching.**
  Don't coach someone and then walk away for three months. Follow up with spot coaching for as long as the person needs you.

Mentoring

A mentor is a person who acts as teacher, coach, counselor, and advisor. Good leaders (and those who are most influential) are almost always mentors for one or more people in their organizations. To be an effective mentor, do the following:

- **Be accessible.**
  Don't build walls between yourself and your team members. Develop clear channels for them to gain access to you.

- **Take an interest in their growth and development.**
  Showing that you care is half the battle. The advice you give may be far less important than the time you take to give it.

- **Help your mentees evaluate their strengths and weaknesses.**
  Teach them first how to be honest about their performance and development needs and then how to grow.

- **Observe their performance regularly and offer constructive suggestions at appropriate moments.**

- **Provide day–to–day coaching (rather than longer–term performance reviews).**
  Give immediate feedback and discuss ways to improve or do the job more effectively.

- **Grow their own insights and independence.**
  Good mentors encourage people to think for themselves and make their own decisions.

- **Let mentees know when they're doing well.**
  Encourage them. Celebrate their accomplishments. Give public recognition.

- **Strive to set a good example.**
  Model all of the behaviors and values that result in productive contributions to the business and active, energetic team membership.

- **Build self-confidence by encouraging risk taking and learning from failure, and rewarding success.**
  Self-confidence is contagious. Once you create a "confident culture," confidence will perpetuate itself.
- **Stimulate people to challenge themselves.**
  If they're in a rut, find out why. Encourage them to change their working conditions or processes to make it more stimulating. If they're complacent, find new challenges for them; involve them in something new and stress its importance; give them a role that demands energy and commitment.
- **Challenge them to keep moving the bar higher.**
  Encourage them to stretch goals and objectives, and show an interest in their careers.
- **Model growth and self-development.**
  Make your own self-development program public and show them the way. Your momentum alone will energize many others, and as they watch you succeed, they will see how to do it themselves.
- **Be continually supportive of others and open to new mentoring relationships.**
  Be willing to help others and provide the guidance they want or need. Don't continue mentoring when it is no longer needed. As your mentees go out "on their own," so to speak, take on new mentees who are eager to benefit from your knowledge and experience.

INFLUENCE Downward

Applying Power and Influence

The relationship between boss and subordinate or leader and team member is one of *reciprocity* and **mutual dependence**. Because both parties depend on one another, a considerable amount of influence is exercised both ways all the time. For both to work together most effectively, each must be able to influence the other and each must be willing, to some extent, to be influenced.

It's easy to see how executives, managers, supervisors, and other leaders influence downward. These "bosses" have role, resource, and information power, and (usually) network and reputation, so they operate with high organizational power. They may also be persuasive, likeable experts. Their techniques can include stating, legitimizing, and even threatening ~ but typically they influence through consulting, logical persuading, appealing to values, and modeling.

Interestingly, subordinates typically use two of these techniques, logical persuading and consulting, to influence upward. A number of factors give subordinates power in their relationships with their bosses:

- Subordinates have skills that are difficult to replace. A leader's power base depends, in part, on how well the team performs.

- Subordinates have special knowledge that others (often including their bosses) lack. The longer people have been in their positions, the more knowledge they acquire. This increases their value (and the boss' dependence).

- Subordinates have support networks their bosses may not have. Because camaraderie tends to develop among subordinates and team members, if one is mistreated, the others may begin to resist or oppose the leader.

- Subordinates know on-the-job shortcuts and have other procedural knowledge that is difficult to replace. The boss may not even know what the shortcuts are.

- Subordinates generally produce products or services that are crucial to the group's performance (and hence the boss' own performance evaluation).

POWER SOURCES IN DOWNWARD INFLUENCE

Effective downward influence (and effective leadership) requires respect for the reciprocal nature of the boss-subordinate relationship and wise use of power and influence. The following seven pages discuss the application of each of the ten power sources and ten influence techniques in downward influence.

POWER SOURCE	APPLICATION IN DOWNWARD INFLUENCE
RESOURCES	Your resource power will typically be higher than that of your subordinates. This is a power source that you need to use freely and liberally, making sure your people have the equipment, space, time, budget, and help from others that they need to do their jobs. Don't just give them what you think they need; ask what they need and, within reason, try to provide it. Withholding of resources in downward influence is self-defeating and detrimental to the organization because of the resource power that subordinates have. Resources must continually flow in both directions in order to accomplish goals.
ROLE	Obviously, your role and the authority you derive from it is your greatest source of power in downward influence. Your role power enables you to make assignments, determine priorities, and control work flow. However, if you are leading effectively, your role is the one power source you should not have to consciously use, except maybe to assist your subordinates cross-functionally (i.e., "pull strings"). By using your other power sources wisely and fairly, you reinforce your role power.

POWER SOURCES IN DOWNWARD INFLUENCE

POWER SOURCE	APPLICATION IN DOWNWARD INFLUENCE
INFORMATION	Information, like resources, is bidirectional and reciprocal. The more useful information you provide, the more you receive. Within the bounds of confidentiality and the dictates of relevance, make sure your people have the information they need to do their jobs. In turn, request information from them. By keeping yourself informed, you show your interest and concern ~ which, ultimately, builds other power sources such as reputation and history. Subordinates often have their own information pipelines and can provide insights and perspectives you can't get from peers. If your people feel that you openly share information with them, they will be more inclined to share information with you. Information, especially that which is considered privileged, can be used as a reward. People value information to which they don't normally have access. You must be careful not to overuse this type of reward, however, because doing so will decrease your information power and may put you or the organization at risk (depending on the type of information you choose to share and with whom).

POWER SOURCE	APPLICATION IN DOWNWARD INFLUENCE
NETWORK	You can use your connections to get your own job done, of course, and to help your subordinates get their jobs done. Network power is particularly helpful when influencing subordinates who don't report to you directly, if your network includes people to whom they do report or others who might have an impact on their job performance or careers. Take care to give credit to those who help you, and say positive things about them to appropriate members of your network. Doing so builds reputation as well as history.
REPUTATION	Your reputation, positive or negative, plays heavily in your relationships with new subordinates or other downward influencees who don't know you personally. Obviously, it helps to have a positive reputation.
KNOWLEDGE	Knowledge is another power source that you should share freely. It is the main power source for successful coaching. The more you are able to delegate because you have transferred your knowledge, the more freedom you have to build your knowledge and move in other directions. In your position, you have likely gained supervisory and political skills that you can share with downward influencees ~ not just to help them advance their careers, but also to help them work more effectively with one another.

POWER SOURCES IN DOWNWARD INFLUENCE

POWER SOURCE	APPLICATION IN DOWNWARD INFLUENCE
EXPRESSIVE-NESS	Expressiveness comes in handy in all facets of supervision ~ giving instructions, communicating goals, addressing groups, and correcting performance problems. High expressiveness is generally a characteristic of the most admired leaders. Take advantage of opportunities to speak before groups, either internal or external. Invite your subordinates or other team members when appropriate ~ not to witness your awesome public speaking skills, but to provide support or to build their networks. If you're uncomfortable with public speaking, consider enrolling in a training program such as Dale Carnegie or one of the many available business presentations seminars. Join Toastmasters.
CHARACTER	Downward influencees who don't trust you are likely to go along with you only because of your role, if at all. Build this power source through modeling. Model ethical behaviors and organization values in your interactions with downward influencees.
ATTRACTION	The same goes for downward influencees who don't like you. This is not to say that all subordinates must like you or that you should try too hard to make them like you. Being accessible, supportive, and cheerful go a long way toward this goal.
HISTORY WITH THE INFLUENCEE	Being consistent is the key to building a solid history with each and every downward influencee. Beware of how your history with one downward influencee may affect another's perceptions of your attitudes and biases. Avoid favoritism. Allow people to try things they haven't tried before. Don't neglect those whom you don't know as well as others. Delegating (the interactive, "win-win" kind) is a good way to build history.

INFLUENCE TECHNIQUE	APPLICATION IN DOWNWARD INFLUENCE
LEGITIMIZING	The inclination to legitimize is strong in hierarchical organizations with top-down communication styles, particularly those in crisis. Overuse of legitimizing tends to cause resentment among downward influencees and to increase negativity throughout the organization. Legitimizing is generally unnecessary with direct reports. If you find yourself using it frequently, perhaps you need to examine your power base and your relationships with downward influencees. The best use of legitimizing is cross-functional, where you have no direct authority over the influencee.
LOGICAL PERSUADING	You may need to use logical persuading cross-functionally or with downward influencees whose expertise in a particular area is greater than yours. Logical persuading also works well in correcting certain performance problems ~ for example, an individual who refuses to cooperate with another department and fails to see the benefit of cooperating. In general, though, logical persuading is a poor choice in downward influence situations. Overusing it reinforces the belief that certain matters, if not all matters, are up for discussion. As with legitimizing, if you find yourself using logical persuading too frequently, you would do well to examine your power base.

DOWNWARD INFLUENCE TECHNIQUES

INFLUENCE TECHNIQUE	APPLICATION IN DOWNWARD INFLUENCE
APPEALING TO RELATIONSHIP	Appealing to relationship is appropriate in downward influence situations where you have no direct authority. However, with your direct reports, appealing to relationship is unnecessary and unwise. This is not to say that you should not cultivate friendly relationships with subordinates; you should. You should not, however, have to appeal to the relationship of a person over whom you have authority.
SOCIALIZING	Socializing is another good technique to use when influencing downward, across functional lines. Limited socializing (particularly empathizing) can be effective in building and maintaining relationships with all downward influencees. Socialize when you can do so without compromising your authority, and take care to socialize with everyone equally.
CONSULTING	In general, it's a good idea to ask people how they feel about things that affect them. However, like logical persuading, too much consulting can create unrealistic expectations. Use it where it won't compromise your authority.
	Consulting is extremely powerful when used for downward influence. It makes people feel that they and their ideas are valuable. Use consulting to highlight little-known or little-used expertise. Use it as a team builder. Encourage downward influencees to consult with others.
	Consulting is also an excellent technique to use in addressing performance problems and complaints. (*So this is a problem. What do you see as the solution?*)

INFLUENCE TECHNIQUE	APPLICATION IN DOWNWARD INFLUENCE
STATING	If you have legitimate authority, most requests to downward influencees require little more than a smile and a polite statement: *Please do this.* Most uses of stating fall at this end of the spectrum. At the other end is the strong statement, the one that puts the pressure on or the one that precedes a threat. The statement is almost always preferable to the threat, so use it as a last resort before threatening. Stating works well in addressing performance problems and handling conflict, used as a way to share perceptions. *(This is how I perceive your behavior. It affects me in the following ways.)*
APPEALING TO VALUES	Appealing to values is the technique of choice for communicating goals and objectives; for inspiring extraordinary efforts in the face of a deadline or crisis; for addressing minor performance problems early on; and, in general, for reminding team members of organizational values and missions. You must be committed to the values you espouse. Don't appeal to values when you don't feel enthusiastic.
MODELING	Modeling, or leading by example, is the one influence technique you should use every day, the best way to encourage excellent performance. Model the behaviors and attitudes you wish for others to emulate. Be consistent. Recognize those who perform well, subtly pointing to them as models for others. Use modeling in your role as coach and mentor to help downward influencees build their skills and knowledge.

DOWNWARD INFLUENCE TECHNIQUES

INFLUENCE TECHNIQUE	APPLICATION IN DOWNWARD INFLUENCE
EXCHANGING	Excessive use of exchanging in downward influence points to a problem with your power base or relationships with influencees. However, on a limited basis, exchanging works well for reestablishing priorities when subordinates express concerns over the workload or when you anticipate resistance, for gaining cooperation across functional lines, and for addressing some performance problems. Be open to exchanges proposed by subordinates, but don't be afraid to refuse or alter the exchange. Know what each downward influencee values, and be aware of all of the currencies of exchange ~ both tangible and intangible.
ALLIANCE BUILDING	In downward influence, alliance building is team building. Use it where you need to get group buy-in. Don't just build alliances for specific purposes. Always encourage your subordinates and other team members to consult with one another and build consensus. Remind them, in subtle ways, of their shared goals and vision. Build an ongoing alliance. If someone comes to you with a large-scale problem, delegate the authority to form a group and develop a solution. (You may wish to offer some guidelines.) You should not have to build an alliance to influence one subordinate or even a group of subordinates.

Upward
INFLUENCE

Upward Influence

Upward influencees may include your boss, your boss' peers, your boss' bosses, those who report to your boss' peers in other functional groups, or those in your organization who have seniority.

These are the steps for upward influence:

1. Understand your boss or team leader and (to the extent that you work with them directly and regularly) other upward influencees.

2. Understand yourself.

3. Build compatible working relationships.

4. Apply power and influence with care.

One's ability to influence upward relies heavily on the ability to influence one's boss or team leader, so this section of the manual focuses primarily on understanding, building a relationship with, and influencing the person to whom you report directly (your boss).

Page 115 lists questions that will help you develop a sound understanding of your boss and his or her expectations, operating style, and strengths and weaknesses. Pages 116 and 117 will help you develop a similar understanding of yourself.

Understanding both your boss and yourself positions you for relationship building, for which you will find suggestions on pages 118 and 119.

Finally, you must understand how power sources and influence techniques work in upward influence. Page 120 lists some things to keep in mind as you use power sources (pp. 121-124) and influence techniques (pp. 125-128).

UNDERSTANDING YOUR BOSS

To develop your understanding of your boss, ask the following kinds of questions:

- What are your boss' goals and objectives? What is he or she trying to achieve? What drives your boss?

- What is your boss' role in the organization? What "masters" does he or she serve? What resources does your boss control or have access to?

- What are your boss' particular talents? What does he or she do really well? Likewise, how is your boss fallible? In what ways is your boss strong and weak? How can you capitalize on the strengths and compensate for the weaknesses?

- What does your boss expect of you? Generally? Specifically? What does your boss expect next week? Next month? Next year? How clear are those expectations? Has your boss told you what he or she expects? Or are you assuming?

- What do you expect in return? What resources (time, budget, equipment, space, assistance, information) do you need to perform your job most effectively? Is your boss aware of your needs and expectations? How have you communicated them? What was the response?

- What are your boss' priorities? Where are the fires that need to be put out? What can be set aside temporarily? What is critically important to your boss? How do your priorities differ? Do they conflict?

- How much trust and respect exist between you? How could you build trust and respect?

- How well do you get along with your boss? What are your boss' MBTI preferences? How well do your preferences match? Where are the points of frustration or conflict? In what ways don't you get along? And what can you do about it?

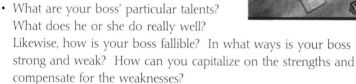

UNDERSTANDING YOURSELF

The next step ~ actually a corollary to the first one ~ is to be sure you understand yourself.

Most people have a firm grasp on their day-to-day goals, priorities, and interactions ~ but they don't give much thought to their overall expectations and operating styles, and they don't understand how those factors affect their interactions with others.

Your Expectations

Your expectations are based on assumptions you make about your job, your boss, and your working environment, and often these assumptions are unconscious as well as unrealistic. Here are some questions to ask:

- What do I expect from my boss? Support? Information? Direction? Coaching? Mentoring? Latitude? Flexibility? Permission? Control? Responsibility? Recognition?

- What kind of working relationship do I expect? Do I expect to be supervised closely or left alone, to do my work and ask for help if I need it?

- What resources do I expect my boss to provide? Time? Budget? Equipment? Software? Books? Space? People?

- What do I expect to provide my boss? What products or services do I expect to deliver?

- How do I expect to communicate with my boss? Through informal chats? Memos? Reports? Phone calls? Presentations? How do I expect my boss to communicate with me?

- What kind of feedback do I expect? When, how much, and in what form do I expect it?

Your Operating Style

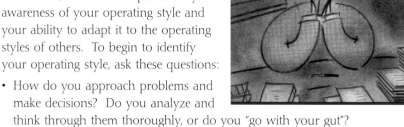

Your ability to work with your boss and all other influencees ~ upward, downward, or lateral ~ depends on your awareness of your operating style and your ability to adapt it to the operating styles of others. To begin to identify your operating style, ask these questions:

- How do you approach problems and make decisions? Do you analyze and think through them thoroughly, or do you "go with your gut"?

- How do you feel most comfortable communicating? In person? On paper? On the phone?

- How do you learn best? By reading, listening, watching, or doing?

- How do you like to work? Do you prefer to work alone or on a team? Are you comfortable delegating or do you feel better doing things yourself?

- What do you like to work on? Are you a detailer or a big picture person? Task oriented? Or people oriented?

- How do you make decisions? Do you need a lot of facts before making a decision? Or are you comfortable with intuition? Do you prefer to make decisions quickly? Or would you rather keep your options open?

- How do you handle your workload? Do you like to plan ahead? Or be spontaneous and open to whatever happens?

- What are your MBTI preferences? Are you an E or an I? S or N? T or F? P or J?

It is helpful to know your MBTI preferences ~ not just from your self-assessment, but from the assessments of others. You know how you see yourself, of course, but to be truly effective you need to know how others see you and how their views differ from yours.

BUILDING A WORKING RELATIONSHIP

The better your relationship with your boss, the more influence you are likely to have ~ not just with your boss, but with other upward influencees as well.

Your boss is only one-half of the relationship. You are the other half, as well as the half over which you have control. To develop an effective working relationship with your boss, take these suggestions:

- **Adjust your operating style to that of your boss.**
  You need to know your operating style and your boss' operating style, and how the two interact. The MBTI can be helpful in this regard.

  Thinking Judgers (ISTJs, INTJs, ESTJs, and ENTJs) fill 70 to 90 percent of the middle and upper management positions in business. The higher you go in an organization, the more Ts and Js you will find.

  If your boss is an INTJ or other J, and you are any kind of P, you may find yourself on the receiving end of frequent pointed comments and lectures about incomplete projects or unmet deadlines, last-minute rushes, temporary solutions, lack of planning, or poor time management. You may feel yourself being pushed to complete your projects, meet your deadlines, and be a better planner/project manager/time manager. You may resist this pushing, focusing instead on your flexibility or your ability to work under pressure. You would do better to push yourself, visibly, toward your boss' goals.

  If you are an extreme F and your boss is a T, you need to understand that your tendency to react emotionally makes your boss uncomfortable ~ which only makes you more emotional because of the negative reaction that you perceive. Your boss may even begin to avoid discussing issues with you because of this.

  Instead of allowing a mismatch of perceptions to limit your career, remind yourself that your boss does not share your emotional view, that it's not as personal or as big a deal to him or her. It's only a matter of solving a problem or getting a job done. In time, you'll find yourself believing this, reacting emotionally less often, and becoming more of a T yourself.

These are only two examples of how people of different operating styles can misunderstand each other and how the misunderstandings can damage relationships. To work effectively with your boss, your operating styles must be compatible (or you must compensate for the differences).

- **Develop a set of mutual expectations.**
  Be sure that you understand your boss' expectations and that you communicate your own. Don't assume that your boss knows your goals and priorities, or vice versa. Talk over your expectations so that both of you know what to expect and when to expect it.

- **Manage the flow of information.**
  Until you achieve a good working relationship, managing the flow of information can be difficult. The key is to provide the right information, in the right amount, in the right way, at the right time. If your boss wants details, provide them. If not, don't. If your boss likes written reports, write them. If not, inform him or her orally, at the right time. If your boss doesn't like to be approached in the hallway, then make an appointment. And so on.

- **Be dependable and straightforward.**
  Your relationship with your boss has to be based on trust, so live up to your commitments. And always be honest and forthcoming. Moreover, you should try to be friendly and cooperative. People who go to work with chips on their shoulders rarely sustain power and influence for very long, no matter how expert they might be.

- **Use the boss' time and resources wisely.**
  Be selective about how much of your boss' time you use. Don't approach your boss with issues you can resolve yourself or invite the boss to meetings that he or she doesn't need to attend.

Upward

APPLYING POWER AND INFLUENCE

In general, knowledge, information, and resources are your primary power sources in influencing your boss or team leader. However, your power sources will vary from situation to situation and will depend on the relationships between you and your colleagues as well as you and your boss.

Once you understand your boss, you need to examine your power sources and your use of influence techniques.

What are your strongest power sources? Which ones do you need to build? Which influence techniques do you generally use with your boss? Which ones work well? Which ones don't work? Which ones could you use more effectively? Which ones should you use more often? Which ones should you avoid? Under what circumstances?

Section 4a discusses the reciprocal nature of power and influence in boss–subordinate relationships. Here, again, are some factors that give you power in influencing your boss:

- You have skills that are difficult to replace (knowledge and resource power).

- You probably have knowledge your boss or team leader doesn't have (knowledge, information, and resource power).

- As a member of the team, you are part of the leader's power base (resource power).

- You have supporters among your colleagues (network power).

- Your boss' or team leader's performance evaluation hinges on what you produce (resource power).

Here's the key point to remember about upward influence: **Your power sources are consumable.** If you call attention to them or use them frequently in other blatant ways, you'll rapidly deplete them. Threatening to quit, for example, is an unwise use of power. It might work once, but it's not likely to work a second time.

When influencing upward, you must use your power sources subtly and continually replenish them. Some power sources, like reputation and history, tend to go away if you don't keep building them.

The next few pages discuss the ten power sources and the ten influence techniques, and their applications in upward influence.

POWER SOURCES IN UPWARD INFLUENCE

POWER SOURCE	APPLICATION IN UPWARD INFLUENCE
RESOURCES	When you're influencing upward, your resource power is typically lower than your boss', but don't underestimate your strengths here. You have knowledge, skills, information, and connections that make you indispensable to your boss. You are a resource.
	You can even use your resource power to "reward" your boss (with earlier project completions, higher-than-expected performance, favorable reviews, and additional or unexpected resources). The simple feeling that you like your boss and enjoy working for him or her is a resource in itself.
	Withholding of resources in this circumstance would include slowing down work, missing deadlines, withholding information or support, giving unfavorable reviews, blocking the boss' efforts, and other kinds of sanctions. These techniques are detrimental to the best interests of the organization, and if you use them you do so at great personal risk. Similarly, you would be unwise to withhold resources from upward influencees other than your boss.
ROLE	Your boss and other upward influencees will probably always have more legitimate authority than you do, and unless you're promoted to a position that puts you in a lateral relationship, there's really no way to increase this source of power except by using the procedural authority that's inherent in your position. If you have to follow procedural rules, for example, then procedure becomes the basis for your authority. However, role is not a good source of power when influencing upward.

Upward

POWER SOURCES IN UPWARD INFLUENCE

POWER SOURCE	APPLICATION IN UPWARD INFLUENCE
INFORMATION	Information is one of the best sources of organizational power when influencing upward (the other one is resources). You can increase your information power by keeping yourself informed and doing your homework. Indeed, you can increase this source of power enough to become virtually indispensable to your boss, provided he or she doesn't have access to, retain, or command the same information.
NETWORK	Network power, like information power, can make you indispensable to your boss. Your ability to get things done through connections enhances your boss' work performance and, ultimately, his or her recognition and rewards. Occasionally, you may be able to build a better relationship by making a connection for your boss.
	When working with upward influencees other than your boss, having their peers in your network is helpful.
REPUTATION	A positive reputation is especially powerful when your relationship with your boss is a new one. On the downside, it tends to increase your new boss' expectations. Once you have established a relationship, your boss may be instrumental in building your reputation by spreading the word of your achievements throughout his or her own network. This helps your power with your boss' bosses and peers.

POWER SOURCE	APPLICATION IN UPWARD INFLUENCE
KNOWLEDGE	Another excellent source of power for upward influence is knowledge. Like information power, expertise can make you indispensable to the operation, and you can build knowledge on your own (self–study), through job experience, and through organizationally sponsored training programs. Performing with excellence gives you tremendous leverage with your boss, and developing your knowledge and expertise is the best way to ensure excellent performance.
EXPRESSIVE–NESS	Expressiveness is another excellent source of power for upward influencing. The more persuasive you are, the more effective you're likely to be when using the most common upward influence technique~ logical persuading. If you're persuasive with your boss, you're likely to be as persuasive with others, and that will make you more valuable as a member of your boss' team, particularly as a liaison to other departments and as a representative of your own department.
ATTRACTION	Attraction is an excellent source of power because it increases your interpersonal attractiveness. This can be problematic with upward influence, however, if your boss feels compromised because of his or her personal feelings toward you, or worse ~ threatened by your charisma. Highly charismatic people tend to be natural leaders, and even bosses aren't immune from that influence. Nonetheless, most bosses allow themselves to be influenced more by people they like, so attraction can be helpful in upward influence.

Upward

POWER SOURCES IN UPWARD INFLUENCE

POWER SOURCE	APPLICATION IN UPWARD INFLUENCE
CHARACTER	Your boss' perceptions of your character are critical not only to your success at influencing your boss, but also to building your remaining power sources. If your boss regards you as trustworthy, he or she is likely to share more information. If your boss perceives a similarity in your personal values, he or she is likely to make connections for you and help you build your network.
HISTORY WITH THE INFLUENCEE	Your history with your boss, once established, is critical not only to your relationship with your boss, but also your relationships with your colleagues and your chances of receiving prime assignments, your access to information or resources, and your ability to influence your boss and other upward influencees. Build history by volunteering for assignments (both from your boss and, with your boss' approval, from other upward influencees), accepting delegated tasks with enthusiasm, and giving positive or constructive feedback on assignments as you receive and complete them.

POWER SOURCE	APPLICATION IN UPWARD INFLUENCE
LOGICAL PERSUADING	This is one of the best techniques to use in upward influence. The key to success is doing your homework and being able to show that you've reached your conclusions logically and have the evidence to back them up. Bosses and other upward influencees need to know why you're making your request, asking for resources, or choosing a particular alternative, and logical persuading is the best technique for giving them that information.
CONSULTING	Consulting is an effective upward influence technique because it engages an upward influencee in the problem and will appeal to his or her ego. Everyone likes to feel needed, and consulting satisfies that need. It also allows the boss to use hard-earned expertise. Beware of using this technique with "hands off" bosses, but with "hands on" bosses it is very effective.
EXCHANGING	Exchanging is an effective upward influence technique, but you have to be very subtle in proposing an exchange with a boss. Explicit bargaining, especially with old-style hierarchical managers, can rapidly lead to resistance or opposition. You usually have to propose an exchange more subtly: "I'd like to move the deadline to Friday. If we can do that, my report could include the off-line transactions we discussed yesterday morning."

Upward

UPWARD INFLUENCE TECHNIQUES

INFLUENCE TECHNIQUE	APPLICATION IN UPWARD INFLUENCE
ALLIANCE BUILDING	Alliance building is often easier with upward influencees other than your boss, particularly if you're working on an interdepartmental project. However, it is a good technique to use with your boss as well. Try to build an alliance by getting your boss (or another manager) to support you in a project whose success would benefit him or her. The key to upward alliance building is to make the alliance attractive by making potential successes highly visible in the organization. Be very careful if your boss is opposed to your influence goal. The influence attempt could backfire if the boss senses that you're "ganging up" on him or her. You can sometimes build alliances among your boss' peers. Here you need to be careful, too, but your influence attempt is more likely to succeed than if you build an alliance among your boss' subordinates.
APPEALING TO VALUES	Appealing to values will be effective to the extent that your boss will be inspired by appeals to tradition, loyalty, customer service, excellence, humanity, and other "inspirations." Generally, the stronger your attraction and expressiveness, the more effective this technique will be. But beware. Unless you're very skilled in the use of this technique, it is risky and could easily fail. Before using this technique, know your boss well enough to know whether it will work. Bosses and other upward influencees don't generally need to be reminded of organizational goals and values, so use appealing to values only to the extent that it highlights your own awareness of those goals and values.

INFLUENCE TECHNIQUE	APPLICATION IN UPWARD INFLUENCE
SOCIALIZING	This technique is usually less effective with bosses unless you have a good personal relationship already established. Even then, you must be careful not to compromise the boss' authority or position. Essentially, it's better to let your boss define the relationship, and if he or she is comfortable with a relationship based on friendship, then socializing can be effective. If the boss is not comfortable with friendship, then don't use this technique. Be careful, too, in socializing with your boss' peers and bosses ~ particularly if your organization is very hierarchical, with a top-down communication style.
APPEALING TO RELATIONSHIP	This technique is worth a try, with the same caveats as for socializing. Be careful of the appearance you convey to your colleagues, who may resent your relationship with the boss. When socializing with your boss' peers and bosses, be careful of the appearance you convey to your boss.
MODELING	Modeling can be an effective upward influence technique~ perhaps more in day-to-day, cumulative influence than in specific influence situations. For example, your boss or another upward influencee may observe your work habits or your behavior toward colleagues, and make positive comments to others. This can only build your power base. Your boss may also be impressed with the results of a suggestion you've made or a method you've used and direct that it be implemented elsewhere or on a larger scale.

Upward Influence Techniques

INFLUENCE TECHNIQUE	APPLICATION IN UPWARD INFLUENCE
LEGITIMIZING	Legitimizing is a difficult technique to use in upward influence. Most bosses are already fully aware of legitimate procedures, rules, laws, etc. They might take offense at being reminded of them. Generally, it's best to use legitimizing more subtly. Request travel on an official company Travel Request form, for example. In your proposal, refer to standard procedures or policy as the basis for your approach or conclusions. That's how to use legitimizing with your boss. Do the same with upward influencees other than your boss.
STATING	This technique is risky, particularly with a boss who is more role oriented. It can be very effective with a boss who respects directness and self-confidence. When your influence goal is critical, another technique~ such as consulting or logical persuading ~ may be a better choice. Use stating with your boss' peers and bosses only when your boss is aware and supportive of your influence goal. With upward influencees other than your boss, stating may work if you and/or your boss have a great deal of organizational power.

Lateral
INFLUENCE

LATERAL INFLUENCE

Lateral influence is, in many respects, the most crucial type of influence ~ particularly in today's flatter, less hierarchical organizations, where you often have to get your work done without having the formal authority to obtain resources or command others. In today's organizations, you need to be able to influence colleagues to cooperate with you, assist or support you, provide resources or information, or in other ways make themselves and their knowledge and skills available to you so you can accomplish your goals. In short, you must be able to influence laterally.

Lateral influence requires, first of all, that you view colleagues as trustworthy and well-intentioned. As Allan Cohen and David Bradford note in *Influence Without Authority*:

> *Effective influence begins with the way you think about those you want to influence. You have already won half the battle when you can see each person, no matter how stubborn and prickly he or she seems to be, as a potential **strategic ally** or **partner**.*

This is not to say that everyone is trustworthy and well-intentioned. But if you assume the worst, you are unlikely to form the kinds of alliances necessary to build lateral influence.

Good relationships are the key to broad lateral influence, and those relationships have to be built on respect, admiration, need, mutual obligation, friendship, and trust.

Here are three steps to achieving broad lateral influence:

1. Identify and assess lateral influencees.

2. Build relationships with lateral influencees.

3. Apply power and influence to gain their cooperation.

Page 131 tells how to identify and assess lateral influencees. Pages 132-134 offer suggestions for building and maintaining a network of collegial relationships necessary to achieve broad lateral influence, and page 135 lists the reasons why some lateral influence attempts are unsuccessful ~ i.e., why some colleagues don't cooperate. Pages 136-138 explain the lateral applications of power sources; pages 139-144, the lateral applications of influence techniques; and pages 145-148, the elements of successful lateral exchange.

ASSESSING LATERAL INFLUENCEES

The first step is to assess your lateral influence needs and lateral influencees. Below is a set of questions you should ask.

- Whom do you need to influence? Whose cooperation do you need to achieve your goals? Who controls the resources and information you need? Who has access to others whose assistance or support you need?

- What are their goals and agendas? What drives them? What do they worry about? What are their primary job concerns?

- How will they view the situation? What stake will they have in it? Why should they care?

- Why should they cooperate or comply? What's in it for them? How does cooperation help them achieve their goals?

- What do they have to contribute? What special knowledge, skills, information, or resources do they possess or control?

- What are their values and priorities? How would they define a "win"? And what could you offer that fits the definition?

- What do you have to give in return? What do you have that they need? What are the rewards for compliance? What are the consequences of noncompliance or noncooperation?

- Where are the areas of similarity between you and them? Where are you alike? Where are you different?

- What risks would they be taking? What rules or traditions would they be breaking? Why shouldn't they cooperate?

- How much support can you reasonably ask them to give?

- What are their operating styles? Their MBTI preferences? Are there any potential personality conflicts? Which influence techniques are likely to succeed?

BUILDING RELATIONSHIPS

The next step is to build relationships with lateral influencees. Your goal is to create a network of positive and productive relationships with a wide range of colleagues throughout your organization. Clearly, you can't do this overnight. Here are some steps:

- **Build your people skills.**
  One way to begin is by reading. Robert Bolton's *People Skills* is an excellent place to begin. Read and practice assertiveness, active listening, and conflict resolution. If you feel relatively unskilled in these areas, and especially if you are an extreme introvert, sign up for training classes.

- **Learn to tolerate differences between yourself and others.**
  Remember that others' attitudes and actions make sense from their points of view, so try to understand the world as others see it. Don't assume the worst; you're probably wrong. Instead, try to view situations as others see them. How does it make sense from another perspective?

  Once you recognize that differences are legitimate, the differences become easier to tolerate.

- **Learn to identify others' operating styles and how they interact with yours, and then compensate.**
  Everyone has a particular operating style, with particular strengths and weaknesses. Some people are outgoing and thrive in social gatherings; others are introverted and more comfortable working alone. Some people focus on details; others prefer the big picture. Some people are analytical and rational; others are intuitive; others are emotional. Some people make quick decisions; others like to keep their options open. Some base their decisions on logic; others on values.

  Note the MBTI preferences of others. If you are a Thinking Introvert, or an I _ T_, and you notice someone who spends a lot of time "hobnobbing" or "flitting around," talking to people about who's doing what and reflecting the mood of the day ~ recognize that this person is probably a Feeling Extravert, or E _ F_. He or she is likely to care less about your plan and how you arrived at it than about how it affects others and how they feel about it. Present your plan accordingly.

Once you tune in to operating styles, and to MBTI preferences in particular, they become easier and easier to spot. You'll quickly learn which influence techniques work with which types in which situations.

- **Focus on strengths, not weaknesses.**

    Look for the strengths of others. If you focus on strengths, you will eventually be able to overlook or work around the weaknesses. Give positive or constructive feedback; don't criticize.

    Never speak negatively about others. Doing so will only damage your reputation and detract from your character power ~ not to mention create a problem when you least expect or need it. Conversely, speaking positively builds power and prevents problems.

- **Get to know your colleagues.**

    First get to know everyone in your own area, and then branch out and get to know colleagues in other areas. Here are some ways to do it:

    * Socialize. Introduce yourself and spend a few minutes learning about them. Meet them for coffee breaks or lunch and talk more about your mutual interests, job concerns, and so on. A relaxed and informal atmosphere is best. Don't miss picnics and parties, especially if your organization is very large. These functions provide prime relationship-building opportunities, as do softball and other sports teams, golf tournaments, and car pools.

    * Sign up for organization-wide training programs and sit next to people you don't know.

    * Volunteer for task forces and other interdepartmental assignments.

    * Invite cross-functional representatives to your planning sessions.

    * Demonstrate an interest in other functional groups. Learn how they operate. Inform them of your plans and ask for their input. Learn as much as you can about their people and their issues, concerns, and priorities.

BUILDING RELATIONSHIPS

- **Discover common interests and create common goals.**
  Find out about your colleagues' backgrounds ~ where they went to school and where they worked before joining your organization. Find out where your colleagues live, how many are in their families, what they like to do in their spare time, etc. (Be appropriate and moderate ~ don't pry.)

  Assume that your cross-functional colleagues share your (or your clients') goals, needs, and issues ~ at least at the organizational level. Communicate these in your requests.

- **Treat them like customers.**
  When colleagues ask you for help, make sure you understand and then go out of your way to satisfy their needs. Ask how satisfied they are and how you can improve your service.

- **Deal directly with poor relationships.**
  If you have a poor relationship with a colleague, confront the issues (not the person) and try to resolve them. If necessary, find a neutral place to sit and talk. Share your perceptions and ask the colleague to share his or hers. Discover the causes of problems and work out mutually acceptable solutions.

- **Resolve conflicts quickly.**
  When conflict arises, try to resolve it quickly. Listen and empathize. Recognize legitimate differences and seek compromise. Depersonalize the conflict by discussing issues and behaviors, not people and personalities. Don't be defensive. Instead, be willing to admit to your misjudgments and mistakes. Seek win-win solutions that preserve relationships.

APPLYING POWER AND INFLUENCE

To be effective in applying power and influence laterally, you must first understand the reasons why colleagues don't cooperate.

Once you understand those reasons and recognize that they are legitimate, you can build the needed power sources and select the most appropriate influence techniques.

Pages 136–144 discuss the lateral applications of power sources and influence techniques.

Why Colleagues Don't Cooperate

1. They have different goals and priorities; they serve their own masters; they have a different view.

2. Their time and resources are limited or already committed.

3. They lack the knowledge or skill; they don't feel qualified.

4. They don't want to take a risk (one you may not be aware of).

5. They disagree with your assessment or approach; they prefer another alternative.

6. They don't understand your needs; they don't know how or why they should comply.

7. Their own needs are not served by complying with you; they have nothing to gain by complying or something to gain by not complying.

8. They don't know you, don't trust you, don't like you, or don't view the relationship in the same way as you do.

9. They can't comply because of ethics, law, policy, procedure, or their bosses' orders.

10. They don't see value in the exchange.

Lateral

POWER SOURCES IN LATERAL INFLUENCE

POWER SOURCE	APPLICATION IN LATERAL INFLUENCE
ROLE	Role power is important to lateral influence in that your role provides you with authority and resources that your colleagues may need. It makes you a more or less valuable member of individual colleagues' networks, and therefore more or less able to get whatever you need from them.
RESOURCES	Resources (people, equipment, space, budget, time, etc.) are currencies of exchange, and exchanging is one of the most-used lateral influence techniques. The more you have of whatever resources your colleagues may need, the more likely you are to be able to negotiate exchanges in your favor. Use your resource power wisely by defining the terms of usage of your resources.
INFORMATION	Information is another currency of exchange. The more you have of the kind your colleagues need or want, the more power you have.
NETWORK	Network power, like resource and information power, can make you invaluable to your colleagues. Your ability to provide them with connections or use your connections to help them can enrich their personal as well as their professional lives. Making a connection for a colleague builds your history with the colleague as well as the person to whom you connect the colleague. It helps to have your colleagues' bosses in your network.

POWER SOURCE	APPLICATION IN LATERAL INFLUENCE
REPUTATION	Needless to say, a positive reputation makes it much easier to influence laterally. Colleagues are not likely to support your causes or grant your requests if you have a negative reputation; they are likely to resist your attempts at relationship building. Your reputation is key to your ability to build relationships and influence others. It is therefore a primary source of power for lateral influence.
KNOWLEDGE	Your knowledge and skills, like resources and information, are currencies of exchange. These give you the ability to assist your colleagues in accomplishing their tasks and to enhance the quality of what they produce. In essence, your knowledge and skills give you the ability to make your colleagues look good.
EXPRESSIVE-NESS	Expressiveness is needed for all influence techniques, but especially for logical persuading and socializing ~ both of which are key lateral influence techniques. The more expressive you are, the better at building relationships and the more persuasive you will be.
ATTRACTION	Attraction is a key power source for lateral influence because of its importance in the preferred lateral influence technique of appealing to relationship and the primary relationship–building influence technique of socializing. You can build this power source by identifying and focusing on commonalities with colleagues. Even those who don't understand or like you at first may come around if you subtly show them the ways in which you are similar to them.

Lateral

Power Sources in Lateral Influence

POWER SOURCE	APPLICATION IN LATERAL INFLUENCE
CHARACTER	Character (or others' perceptions of your character) is key to your ability to build relationships with colleagues ~ particularly those who are Feelers and Judgers. The way to build this power source is to be ethical, fair, and consistent in all of your interactions ~ personal and professional. Doing so builds your reputation at the same time.
HISTORY WITH THE INFLUENCEE	History is perhaps the most critical of all power sources for lateral influence. If you have no history, you have no relationship. The way to build this power source is to build positive relationships with as many people as you possibly can. This builds your network power as well.

INFLUENCE TECHNIQUE	APPLICATION IN LATERAL INFLUENCE
	If you have built a solid network of collegial relationships throughout your organization, you may need to do nothing more than ask friends for help or favors. Appealing to relationship is therefore the technique of choice for lateral influence ~ which is not to say that you should always appeal to relationship. Choose techniques that are appropriate to each influence situation, using appealing to relationship sparingly with individual colleagues but liberally with colleagues across the board.
APPEALING TO RELATIONSHIP	Appealing to relationship sets up an exchange in that asking for a favor obligates you to return the favor at some point in the future. Keep this in mind. Know what you are willing to exchange, and don't ask for more than you can give.
SOCIALIZING	Even if you don't have an existing relationship with a colleague, you can ask for a favor as a way to start building the relationship. (Just be sure to reciprocate when the time comes.) This is the way to use socializing when you need something right away. Otherwise, use socializing to build relationships with colleagues you don't know very well. Empathize. Identify shared interests and other commonalities. Invite colleagues to lunch.

Lateral

LATERAL INFLUENCE TECHNIQUES

INFLUENCE TECHNIQUE	APPLICATION IN LATERAL INFLUENCE
CONSULTING	People are more likely to support something if they are included in it in some way. When you ask for others' input *and then use their ideas in some way that they can see,* you have made them, in effect, co-authors of the idea, and they will be more likely to support it. One subtle way to reinforce this idea is to shift your reference to the idea from *I* to *we.* When you first approach them, speak of the idea as *my idea.* Then, after incorporating their input, speak of it as *our proposal.* This invokes the macro technique of alliance building.
	The technique of consulting is a powerful relationship builder in that it shows colleagues you value their expertise, ideas, and support. When you first approach a lateral influencee you don't know, socialize ~ then consult.
LOGICAL PERSUADING	Logical persuading is a good technique to use in any direction, but with colleagues, it is important to establish credibility first. Don't assume that colleagues know your qualifications or that they perceive you as an expert in the target area. Explain, if you need to.
	If you're trying to influence another expert in the target area, then be sure to test your own assumptions first and bring enough credible, documented evidence to support your case. Most technical colleagues will expect to be able to verify your conclusions themselves. If you lack the evidence, you will lose credibility quickly.
	People tend to be persuaded by what they already believe to be true.
	(Continued)

INFLUENCE TECHNIQUE	APPLICATION IN LATERAL INFLUENCE
LOGICAL PERSUADING (Continued)	Your chances of success are higher if you know what the influencee already believes and can incorporate the existing beliefs into your argument. Additionally, if you construct your argument so that it appears logical (by breaking it down and enumerating the parts in some order), most people will be influenced to some degree ~ regardless of the content.
APPEALING TO VALUES	Appealing to values works well cross–functionally when cooperation serves some higher ideal such as quality, customer service, speed, innovation, etc. This technique can also be used in solving problems and resolving conflict ~ for example, telling stories that illustrate similar problems and how they were solved, or appealing to the values of two colleagues who are not getting along. In the latter instance, you must know the values of the individuals.
MODELING	Modeling can be an effective lateral influence technique~ perhaps more in building one's power base and overall ability to influence than in specific influence situations. For example, modeling professionalism (dress, punctuality, work ethic, responsiveness, etc.) increases your colleagues' perceptions that you are an influential person, a leader, a force to be reckoned with. This builds your reputation and increases the likelihood that colleagues will comply with your requests and support your causes.

(Continued)

LATERAL INFLUENCE TECHNIQUES

INFLUENCE TECHNIQUE	APPLICATION IN LATERAL INFLUENCE
MODELING (Continued)	Modeling is an everyday leadership tool. In a crisis, it helps to keep colleagues focused and energetic, and to turn the situation around more quickly. Model a positive attitude; do what needs to be done; accentuate the positive, and help others do the same.
ALLIANCE BUILDING	Alliance building is an effective ~ but little used ~ lateral influence technique. Build alliances when you need broad support among colleagues, either across functional lines or within your functional group. Begin with the most visible and influential people.
	Alliance building is another everyday leadership tool and a network builder. By taking the initiative to build an alliance, for whatever purpose, you demonstrate leadership. With each colleague, you build a relationship that is in itself an alliance. By strengthening your alliances, you strengthen your network.
STATING	Stating is assertive, and therefore useful in a wide range of situations that call for assertiveness. Stating works well for making polite requests to colleagues who are likely to comply because of shared goals or friendly relationships. Others, especially those who don't know you, might perceive your use of stating as pushy and question or refuse your request. Use strong statements only when you are not concerned about the relationship.

INFLUENCE TECHNIQUE	APPLICATION IN LATERAL INFLUENCE
LEGITIMIZING	Colleagues are more likely to respond to requests that look or sound official, but legitimizing ~ either on paper or in person ~ tends to depersonalize the influence attempt. Techniques such as appealing to relationship, socializing, consulting, exchanging, and alliance building are much more personal and therefore conducive to relationship building, even if you use them over the phone. Refer to policy, procedure, tradition, management, etc., when appropriate ~ especially when you have no relationship. But be careful not to overuse this technique. Doing so diminishes its effectiveness as well as your power base.
EXCHANGING	When you don't have an existing relationship with the influencee and don't have time to build one, exchanging is often the technique of choice. It is based on the principle of reciprocity. In friendships, reciprocity is unspoken and assumed; in exchanging, reciprocity is negotiated. In effect, I offer to do something for you if you'll do something for me. In practice, exchanges are often very subtle.
	Successful exchanges benefit both parties and tend to build the relationship. So a period of exchanging with a colleague will likely create a stronger personal relationship, and over time the technique of choice might shift from exchanging to appealing to relationship.
	As children, we learn to exchange goods and services. We perfect this skill as adults through education and experience in negotiation.

(Continued)

Lateral

LATERAL INFLUENCE TECHNIQUES

INFLUENCE TECHNIQUE	APPLICATION IN LATERAL INFLUENCE
EXCHANGING (Continued)	Exchanges occur daily and are often subtle and informal. A waiter exchanges a smile and good service for a larger tip. A busy receptionist exchanges courtesy for the waiting caller's patience. At a service counter, we fill out the forms properly and completely in exchange for expedited service.

Indeed, most of what we exchange is intangible: faster response, support at the next meeting, courtesy, patience, understanding, acceptance. We may even exchange things for others' perceptions of us as nice people and for our own good feelings about ourselves. Giving to charities and doing volunteer work are good examples of such exchanges.

In *Influence Without Authority*, Allan Cohen and David Bradford refer to the goods and services we exchange with one another as the currencies of exchange, and that seems an appropriate metaphor. We always exchange something of value (the currency), but that something does not need to be tangible.

A list of the currencies of lateral exchange begins on page 146.

UNDERSTANDING LATERAL EXCHANGE

Because lateral relationships are inherently equal, neither person is compelled to be influenced by the other. There usually is no significant power differential, and colleagues generally do not have to cooperate with one another unless they wish to. Consequently, lateral exchange is a common method of influence among people on the same level in an organization.

All of this sounds more manipulative than it actually is. Most lateral cooperation is the result of implicit agreements among colleagues to cooperate. Even though we believe we're being cooperative out of goodwill and camaraderie, we are actually agreeing to reciprocate that goodwill. Note what happens when a colleague becomes uncooperative. That person fails to reciprocate the goodwill extended by others and soon loses their goodwill.

Exchanging is based on the psychological concept of reciprocation, which means that we agree, usually implicitly, to reciprocate favors given to us by others. These factors do not need to be tangible. We usually reciprocate when someone greets us.

Hi, how are you this morning?
Fine, how are you?

Even this simple **exchange** is an example of reciprocation. If people (especially colleagues) did not reciprocate, cooperation would break down and we would be unable to form effective social groups.

So think of exchange as a means of getting along, of cooperating with one another so each of us can accomplish his or her tasks and goals.

To exchange laterally, we need to have something the other person values. We refer to these things as the "currencies of lateral exchange," and tables listing common currencies appear on the next three pages.

Often, when two colleagues exchange, the currencies are unspoken and understood. Most people prefer the currencies of exchange to remain unspoken. However, when the other person is less willing to exchange, you may need to make these currencies clear, conscious, and tangible. Generally speaking, the less cooperative the influencee is, the more explicit your bargaining must be.

Lateral

THE CURRENCIES OF LATERAL EXCHANGE

The issue, for uncooperative colleagues, is *What's in it for me?* The following tables will help you identify what you can offer in exchange for that person's cooperation.

Professional Satisfaction

- Participation in a high-profile project or important effort for the organization
- Achievement of a key organization goal
- Membership on a task force or team working on an interesting problem
- The ability to work with specific people or clients
- The ability to focus on what one does best
- The opportunity to excel
- Access to a choice assignment

Task Facilitation

- Quicker response to requests
- Movement or meeting of a deadline
- Relief from an undesirable task or responsibility
- The opportunity to devote more time to critical problems
- The willingness of others to consult or collaborate on or solve one's problems
- The willingness of others to review one's work and give positive feedback
- Flexibility in procedures, policies, or rules
- Administrative/technical assistance

Recognition

- Formal recognition for one's efforts/contributions
- Informal acknowledgment of one's contributions, especially in the presence of significant people, like the boss
- Receipt of or recommendation for an award
- Expressions of appreciation or gratitude

- Being thought of positively (as a true professional, team player, problem solver, etc.)
- Being seen as a leader or innovator
- A recommendation for promotion or transfer to a choice assignment or team

Growth

- The opportunity to engage in challenging tasks, ones that stretch one's capabilities
- The opportunity to learn new skills, acquire knowledge, develop one's capabilities
- Participation in a training course or other program that promotes growth
- The opportunity to learn from someone more knowledgeable or experienced; your willingness to be a mentor

Inclusion

- Membership in a particular group
- An invitation or recommendation to participate in a special program
- An invitation to attend a special meeting
- One's name appearing on the distribution list of an important piece of correspondence
- Co-authorship of a key report
- An invitation to participate in a special presentation to important people
- The opportunity to consult on important issues
- An introduction to key people or an invitation to join an inner circle

Lateral

THE CURRENCIES OF LATERAL EXCHANGE

Networking

- The opportunity to extend one's network
- Participation on a task force with executives from around the organization
- The ability to meet or socialize with others in the organization; the opportunity to build a network of colleagues
- The opportunity to develop better relationships with the people in one's network

Resource Access

- Control of more resources
- Access to or receipt of resources ~ time, budget, space, equipment, people, etc.
- Access to more of a particular kind of information
- Assistance in locating and obtaining resources
- Assistance or support on a task or project

Personal Satisfaction

- The opportunity to relax more, take a vacation, have a day off, relieve stress
- Access to someone who will listen and empathize
- The opportunity to remain in or go to a choice location
- Intellectual, emotional, or spiritual stimulation
- The ability to repay a debt
- More freedom/independence
- Greater safety or security
- The feeling that one is being heard
- The feeling that one matters, that one is important
- Enhanced self-image or ego gratification
- The opportunity to develop a relationship; the satisfaction of helping a friend

ASSESSING YOUR INFLUENCE EFFECTIVENESS

To help you assess and increase your effectiveness in the lateral, upward, and downward uses of the various influence techniques, Lore offers the **Survey of Influence Effectiveness** (SIE).

What It Is

The SIE is a multidimensional survey that gives you a better idea of how effectively you influence others, including (1) how frequently you use different influence techniques, (2) how effectively you use those techniques, (3) your sources of power, and (4) your skill in using the influence techniques. The SIE is available as a component of Lore's *Leadership Through Influence* course and as an independent individual assessment.

How It Works

The SIE questionnaire includes about 125 questions on your influencing behaviors and related skills, power base, role, and culture. You and selected others who work with you (including your boss, colleagues, and direct reports) complete the questionnaires and return them to Lore. Lore processes the questionnaires and delivers a detailed feedback report of the responses.

What It Tells You

The SIE feedback report provides a great deal of useful information, including recommendations from the others who completed the questionnaires. You'll learn which techniques your boss, colleagues, and direct reports believe you should use more or less often. You'll also be able to compare how you see yourself with how others see you.

Comparing your scores for technique frequency, effectiveness, and appropriateness will tell you:

- Which techniques you use frequently but ineffectively
- Which techniques you use infrequently but effectively
- The frequency with which you use techniques that may be inappropriate to your position or the culture in which you work

Finally, you'll see how your scores compare to the norms for other survey respondents.

For more information about the SIE or the *Leadership Through Influence* course, call Lore at 970-385-4955.

Lateral

RECOMMENDED READINGS

Understanding the Types

Benfari, Robert. *Understanding Your Management Style: Beyond the Myers-Briggs Type Indicator.* NY: Lexington Books, 1991.

Bolton, Robert and Bolton, Dorothy Grover. *Social Style/Management Style: Developing Productive Work Relationships.* NY: American Management Association, 1984.

Jung, C.G. *Psychological Types.* Princeton: Princeton University Press, 1971.

Hirsh, Sandra Krebs. *Using the Myers-Briggs Type Indicator in Organizations, 2nd Ed.* Palo Alto: Consulting Psychologists Press, Inc., 1991.

Keirsey, David. *Portraits of Temperament.* Del Mar, CA: Prometheus Nemesis Book Company, 1987.

Keirsey, David and Bates, Marilyn. *Please Understand Me: Character & Temperament Types.* Del Mar, CA: Prometheus Nemesis Book Company, 1984.

Kroeger, Otto, with Thuesen, Janet M. *Type Talk at Work: How the 16 Personality Types Determine Your Success on the Job.* NY: Delacorte Press, 1992.

Lawrence, Gordon. *People Types & Tiger Stripes: A Practical Guide to Learning Styles, 2nd Ed.* Gainesville, FL: Center for Applications of Psychological Type, 1979.

Myers, Isabel Briggs and McCaulley, Mary H. *A Guide to the Development and Use of the Myers-Briggs Type Indicator.* Palo Alto: Consulting Psychologists Press, Inc., 1985.

Sharp, Daryl. *Personality Types: Jung's Model of Typology.* Toronto: Inner City Books, 1987.

Influencing with Integrity

Ansari, M.A. and Kapoor, A. "Organizational context and upward influence techniques," *Organizational Behavior and Human Decision Processes,* 1987, 40, 39–40.

Cialdini, Robert B. *Influence: The New Psychology of Modern Persuasion.* NY: Quill, 1984.

Cohen, Allan R. and Bradford, David L. *Influence without Authority.* NY: John P. Wiley & Sons, 1990.

Erez, M. and Rim, Y. "The relationship between goals, influence tactics, and personal and organizational variables," *Human Relations,* 1982, 35, 871–8.

Erez, M., Rim, Y., and Keider, I. "The two sides of the tactics of influence: agent vs. target," *Journal of Occupational Psychology,* 1986, 59, 25–39.

Filley, A.C. and Grimes, A.J. "The bases of power in decision processes," *Academy of Management Proceedings, 27th Annual Meeting,* pp. 133-60.

French, J.R.P. and Raven, B. "The bases of social power," in Cartwright, D., ed., *Studies in Social Power.* Ann Arbor: Institute for Social Research, University of Michigan, 1959, pp. 150-67.

Kipnis, D. and Costentino, J. "Uses of leadership powers in industry," *Journal of Applied Psychology,* 1969, 53, 460-6.

Kipnis, D. and Schmidt, S.M. *Profile of Organizational Influence Strategies.* San Diego: University Associates, 1982.

Kipnis, D. and Schmidt, S.M. "An influence perspective on bargaining within organizations," in Bazerman, M.H. and Roy, J.L., eds. *Bargaining Inside Organizations.* Beverly Hills, CA: Sage, 1983, pp. 303-19.

Kipnis, D. and Schmidt, S.M. "Upward influence styles: relationship with performance evaluation, salary, and stress," *Administrative Science Quarterly,* 1988, 33, 528-42.

Kipnis, D., Schmidt, S.M., and Wilkinson, I. "Intraorganizational influence tactics: explorations in getting one's way," *Journal of Applied Psychology,* 1980, 65, 440-52.

Kotter, John P. *Power and Influence: Beyond Formal Authority.* NY: The Free Press, 1985.

Michener, A. and Schwertfeger, M. "Liking as a determinant of power tactic preference," *Sociometry,* 1972, 35, 190-202.

Mowday, R. "The exercise of upward influence in organizations," *Administrative Science Quarterly,* 1978, 23, 137-56.

Pratkanis, Anthony and Aronson, Elliot. *Age of Propaganda: The Everyday Use and Abuse of Persuasion.* NY: W. H. Freeman and Company, 1991.

Schein, V.E. "Individual power and political behavior," *Academy of Management Review,* 1977, 2, 64-72.

Strauss, G. "Techniques of lateral relationships: the purchasing agent," *Administrative Science Quarterly,* 1962, 7, 161-86.

Yukl, G. and Falbe, C.M. "Influence tactics and objectives in upward, downward, and lateral influence attempts," *Journal of Applied Psychology,* 1990, 75, 132-40.

Yukl, G. *Leadership in Organizations, 2nd Ed.* Englewood Cliffs, NJ: Prentice-Hall, 1989

INDEX

Alliance building	15,16,61–64
by MBTI type	88–89
cautions for	64
conflicting techniques	61
downward application of	112
how to recognize	62
how to recognize people who respond to	62–63
how to use	64
lateral application of	142
power sources for	61
skills for	61
supporting techniques	61
upward application of	126
when to use	63–64
Appealing to relationship	14,33–36
by MBTI type	88–89
cautions for	36
conflicting techniques	33
downward application of	110
how to recognize	34
how to recognize people who respond to	34
how to use	35–36
lateral application of	139
power sources for	33
skills for	33
supporting techniques	33
upward application of	127
when to use	35
Appealing to values	15,49–52
by MBTI type	88–89
cautions for	52
conflicting techniques	49
downward application of	111
how to recognize	50
how to recognize people who respond to	50
how to use	52
lateral application of	141
power sources for	49
skills for	49
supporting techniques	49
upward application of	126

Appealing to values (continued)

    when to use   51

Applying power and influence   80

Asking   16

Assessing lateral influencees   131

Assessing your influence effectiveness   149

Attraction   19,67,76

    downward application of   108

    lateral application of   137

    upward application of   123

Avoiding   17,18

Boss, understanding your   115

Boss–subordinate relationship, the   104

Briggs, Katharine   82

Building relationships with lateral influencees   132–134

Building relationships with upward influencees   118–119

Character   19,67,75

    downward application of   108

    lateral application of   138

    upward application of   124

Coaching and mentoring   101–103

Colleagues, why they don't cooperate   135

Consulting   14,41–44

    by MBTI type   88–89

    cautions for   44

    conflicting techniques   41

    downward application of   110

    how to recognize   41–42

    how to recognize people who respond to   42

    how to use   43–44

    lateral application of   140

    power sources for   41

    skills for   41

    supporting techniques   41

    upward application of   125

    when to use   43

Core concepts of influence   8–9

Correlations, technique/power/skill   20–21

Countering negative techniques   18

Currencies of lateral exchange   146–148

Delegating   98–100

Direction of influence, considering the   80

INDEX

Directional applications of power	78
Downward influence, overview of	94
Downward influencees, empowering	95–97
Effectiveness, assessing your	149
Empowering downward influencees	95–97
Exchange, currencies of lateral	146–148
Exchange, lateral	145
Exchanging	15,16,57–60
by MBTI type	88–89
cautions for	60
conflicting techniques	57
downward application of	112
how to recognize	58
how to recognize people who respond to	58–59
how to use	60
lateral application of	144
power sources for	57
skills for	57
supporting techniques	57
upward application of	125
when to use	59
Explaining	16
Expressiveness	19,67,74
downward application of	108
lateral application of	137
upward application of	123
Extraverts	84,87
Feelers	85,87
History with the influencee	19,67,77
downward application of	108
lateral application of	138
upward application of	124
How people are influenced	24
How to build power sources	68,69,70,71,72,73,74,75,76,77
Influence effectiveness, assessing your	149
Influence strategies	16
Influence techniques	12,13,14,15,16,24–64
choosing	24
downward applications of	109–112
lateral applications of	139–144
negative	17–18
upward applications of	125–128
upward/lateral/downward application summary	92

Influence, core concepts of   8–9
   unethical   6
Influencing by MBTI type   88–89
Influencing by temperament   90–91
Influencing directionally   92
Information   19,66,70
   downward application of   106
   lateral application of   136
   upward application of   122
Inspiring   16
Integrity, the test of   18
Intimidating   17,18
Introverts   84,87
Intuitors   84,87
Judgers   86,87
Knowledge   19,67,73
   downward application of   107
   lateral application of   137
   upward application of   123
Lateral exchange   145
   currencies of   146–148
Lateral influence, overview of   130
Lateral influencees, assessing   131
Lateral influencees, building relationships with   132–134
Legitimizing   13,25–28
   by MBTI type   88–89
   cautions for   28
   conflicting techniques   25
   downward application of   109
   how to recognize   25
   how to recognize people who respond to   26
   how to use   26–28
   lateral application of   143
   power sources for   25
   skills for   25
   supporting techniques   19
   upward application of   128
   when to use   26
Logical persuading   8,23–32
   by MBTI type   88–89
   cautions for   32
   conflicting techniques   29
   downward application of   109

INDEX

Logical persuading (continued)

how to recognize	30
how to recognize people who respond to	30–31
how to use	31–32
lateral application of	141
power sources for	29
skills for	29
supporting techniques	29
upward application of	125
when to use	31

Macro technique (alliance building)	15,16,61–64
Manipulating	88–89
MBTI type, influencing by	101–103
Mentoring, coaching and	95–97
Modeling	15,53–56
by MBTI type	88–89
cautions for	56
conflicting techniques	53
downward application of	111
how to recognize	54
how to recognize people who respond to	54
how to use	55–56
lateral application of	141-142
power sources for	53
skills for	53
supporting techniques	53
upward application of	127
when to use	55

Myers, Isabel Briggs	82
Myers–Briggs Type Indicator® (MBTI®)	82,83
Negative techniques	17–18
countering	18
Network	19,66,71
downward application of	107
lateral application of	136
upward application of	122
Operating styles, understanding	80,82
Organizational power, sources of	12,13,19,66,68–72
Perceivers	86,87
Personal power, sources of	12,13,19,67,73–77
Power and influence, applying	80
Power base	19

Power sources, correlations to influence techniques   20,21
   downward applications of   105–108
   lateral applications of   136–138
   organizational   12,13,19
   personal   12,13,19
   upward applications of   121–124
Power, directional applications of   78
   sources of   66–67,68,69,70,71,72,73,74,75,76,77
   upward/lateral/downward application summary   78
Reciprocity, downward influence and   104
   upward influence and   120
Relationships, building with lateral influencees   132–134
   building with upward influencees   118–119
Reputation   19,66,72
   downward application of   107
   lateral application of   137
   upward application of   122
Resources   19,66,69
   downward application of   105
   lateral application of   136
   upward application of   121
Role   19,66,68
   downward application of   105
   lateral application of   136
   upward application of   121
Sensors   84,87
Situation, understanding the   80,81
Skills   12,13
   correlations to influence techniques   21
Socializing   14,37–40
   by MBTI type   88,89
   cautions for   40
   conflicting techniques   37
   downward application of   110
   how to recognize   37–38
   how to recognize people who respond to   38
   how to use   39–40
   lateral application of   139
   power sources for   37
   skills for   37
   supporting techniques   37
   upward application of   127
   when to use   39

INDEX

Stating	15,16,45–48
by MBTI type	88–89
cautions for	48
conflicting techniques	45
downward application of	111
how to recognize	45
how to recognize people who respond to	46
how to use	47–48
lateral application of	142
power sources for	45
skills for	45
supporting techniques	45
upward application of	128
when to use	46
Strategies	16
Survey of Influence Effectiveness (SIE)	149
Technique/power/skill correlations	20–21
Temperament, influencing by	90–91
Thinkers	85,87
Threatening	17,18
TOPS formula	12,13
Types, influencing different	87–89
Understanding why colleagues don't cooperate	135
Understanding your boss	115
Understanding yourself	116–117
Unethical influence	6
Upward influence, overview of	114
Upward influencees, building relationships with	118–119
Why colleagues don't cooperate	135
Yourself, understanding	116–117